So You Think You Know
PREMIER LEAGUE
FOOTBALL?

TOWER HAMLETS COLLEGE
Learning Centre
Poplar High Street
LONDON
E14 0AF

Clive Gifford

h

© Copyright Hodder Children's Books 2004

Published in Great Britain in 2004
by Hodder Children's Books

Editor: Isabel Thurston
Design by Fiona Webb
Cover design: Hodder Children's Books

10 9 8 7 6 5 4 3

ISBN: 0340 88190 9

Printed by Bookmarque Ltd, Croydon, Surrey

The paper and board used in this paperback by
Hodder Children's Books are natural recyclable products
made from wood grown in sustainable forests. The
manufacturing processes conform to the environmental
regulations of the country of origin.

Hodder Children's Books
a division of Hodder Headline Limited
338 Euston Road
London NW1 3BH

CONTENTS

II TRODUCTIO

So you think you know all there is to know about the Premier League, its teams, players, grounds and history? Reckon you can recall each and every club's highs and lows, the record victories and defeats, the great players, upsets and drama? This book contains over 1000 questions covering all aspects of the Premier League from its formation in 1992 up to the beginning of 2004. Good luck with tackling as many as you can.

About the author

Clive Gifford is an author of more than 60 books for children and adults. Many of these are on sports, including *The Olympics, Drugs And Sport, Football: The Ultimate Guide To The Beautiful Game, Soccer Tactics* and *Super Activ Football*. Clive is Deputy Editor of *AKUTRs* fanzine, a contributor to a number of football magazines and a lifelong supporter of QPR. He has also written more than a dozen quiz books including the *So You Think You Know* series covering topics such as Harry Potter, The Simpsons and David Beckham.

To Anthony, Iola, Finbarr, Batty, Big Mal and Erky for their support.

9 In which year did the Premier League kick off: 1990, 1992 or 1994?

10 Which former Manchester United mid-fielder has managed two Premier League teams, Coventry City and Southampton?

11 What word, beginning with the letter 'v', is given to a shot made with the ball in mid-air?

12 Which footballing superstar left the Premier League in 2003 to play in Spain?

13 And what was the name of the Spanish club he joined?

14 Can you name either of the Premier League teams with the word 'Wanderers' in their name?

15 In the first years of the Premier League two teams were relegated each year: true or false?

16 Which French striker joined Manchester United in January 2004: Louis Saha, Nicolas Anelka or Thierry Henry?

TAP-INS

1. How many teams are there in the 2003/04 Premier League?

2. How many teams were relegated to Division One in 2002/03?

3. Which team has won the Premier League more times than any other?

4. For which Premier League team did Wayne Rooney start his career?

5. Highbury is the ground of which Premier League team?

6. Which Premier League club was taken over by a Russian billionaire in 2003?

7. Who is the longest serving Premier League manager at one club?

8. Which football team plays its home games at Anfield?

17 Which Premier League team's stadium is called White Hart Lane?

18 Which two teams contest the Merseyside Derby?

19 What was the name of Arsenal's first non-British manager?

20 Which team from the south coast of England played its first ever Premier League games in 2003?

21 How many teams were there in the first Premier League: 18, 20, 22 or 24?

22 Which pair of brothers has played for Manchester United for many seasons?

23 Can you name the one former Premier League team with a day of the week in its name?

24 Which Premier League team is known by the nickname 'the Saints'?

25 Which Premier League player was England's leading goal scorer in the 2002 World Cup finals?

26 How many goals are scored in a hat-trick?

27 How many goals have been let in, if a goalkeeper or team are described as having a clean sheet?

28 Who was the club captain of Manchester United in the 2003/04 season?

29 Kenny Dalglish, Alan Hansen and Ian Rush are all famous past players of which Premier League club?

30 How many substitutes can be made in a Premier League match?

31 Which football club plays its matches at Old Trafford?

32 Goalkeepers are allowed to play the ball with their feet, legs and head when outside their penalty area: true or false?

33 For which country does Patrick Viera play his international football?

34 Which former Premier League team moved from South London to Milton Keynes in 2003?

35 Which two teams contest the North London Derby?

36 At which club's ground did England qualify for the 2002 World Cup with a last gasp free kick by David Beckham?

37 And who was the game against: Greece, Germany or Turkey?

38 Underarm, overarm and javelin are all types of free kick moves, throw-in styles or goalkeeper's throws?

39 Tony Adams, Ian Wright and Marc Overmars are all famous past players for which Premier League team?

40 Stamford the Lion is the mascot of which London-based Premier League club?

41 What is the name of the restart where one player from each team competes for the football held and released by the referee?

42 Who is the only player to score more than 200 Premier League goals: Thierry Henry, Alan Shearer, Michael Owen or Dwight Yorke?

43 Which French striker played for both Leeds United and Manchester United?

44 From what country does Ruud van Nistelrooy come?

45 Which football team is known as 'the Dons': Bolton Wanderers, Wimbledon or Southampton?

46 If Fulham are playing at home, what is the main colour of their shirts?

47 For a goal to be scored, does more than half the ball or all of the ball have to be over the line?

48 Which football team is known by the nickname of 'Pompey'?

49 What is the full name of the former Premier League club known as QPR?

50 Which Premier League player's injured toe dominated sports stories in the run-up to England's bid for success at the 2002 World Cup?

REGULAR SEASON

1 Which team won the 1994/95 Premier League?

2 What is the full name of the team known as WBA?

3 Which former Chelsea, and now Southampton, defender is one of the few Premier League and England footballers to have an 'x' in his name?

4 Only two managers have managed one team for the entire duration of the Premier League. Sir Alex Ferguson is one; can you name the other?

5 Which Premier League team was managed by Dr Josef Venglos for a spell in the 1990s?

6   At the start of the 1996/97 season, who were the two first-choice strikers for Newcastle United?

7   Which former Premier League team plays at Highfield Road?

8   David Bentley, Sebastian Svard and Jeremie Aliadiere are lesser known players in which Premier League team's squad?

9   Which team only averaged 8391 spectators per game in the first year of the Premier League?

10   What season saw a change to the rules, allowing players to score directly from the kick-off?

11   Which Australian Premier League footballer won the PFA Young Player of the Year award in 2000?

12   At the very start of 2004, who was in fourth place in the Premier League?

13   Which player has scored over 150 Premier League goals, second only to Alan Shearer?

14 Which Tottenham Hotspur player scored more penalties in the 2002 World Cup than any other footballer?

15 Which former Middlesbrough manager became manager of Bradford City in the winter of 2003?

16 Which team let in 93 goals in the 1994/95 season?

17 Which former Premier League team's nickname is 'the Eagles'?

18 Who was the Premier League's top scorer in the 2000/01 season: Kevin Phillips, Thierry Henry or Alan Shearer?

19 Which striker from Ghana quickly became a favourite at Leeds United and scored the 1996 Match of the Day Goal of the Season with a thumping volley against Liverpool?

20 Which Premier League side played 20 cup matches in the 2002/03 season, winning the Intertoto Cup?

21 Which team won the 1994/95 Premier League title on the last day of the season?

22 Paul Durkin, Paul Alcock, Uriah Rennie. What links these three men?

23 Nottingham Forest were unbeaten for 25 games in 1995 before they lost to Blackburn Rovers by the score 2-0, 4-0, 6-0 or 7-0?

24 Nigerian footballing legend Jay Jay Okocha has played in the Premier League for which club?

25 Was Sir Alex Ferguson born in 1938, 1941, 1945 or 1952?

26 What nationality is Aston Villa's 1994/95 leading goal scorer, Dean Saunders?

27 Which Premier League player scored the most goals in the finals of the 2002 World Cup?

28 What two colours are the vertical stripes on Blackburn's home shirts?

29 The most money Leicester City have ever got for a player is £11 million, but for which striker?

30 Which football team plays its football at the Hawthorns?

31 In October 2003, which team thumped Bolton Wanderers, 6-2?

32 Who became the first non-British manager to win the Premier League?

33 To which Nationwide league team was the young David Beckham loaned in the 1990s?

34 Rugby Union star Jonny Wilkinson used to play for the Newcastle United youth team: true or false?

35 James Milner became the youngest ever Premier League goal scorer when he fired home a 2002 goal against West Ham United, Sunderland or Manchester City?

36 Which team averaged the most spectators in the 1999/2000 season: Sunderland or Arsenal?

37 Alan Shearer was the Premier League's leading goal scorer in the 1994/95 season but which club was he playing for?

38 In which year did the bottom-placed team in the Premier League finish a record 25 points short of safety?

39 And which team holds that dubious record?

40 Which club opened its new Walkers Stadium in 2002?

41 Which Premier League team has appeared in Charity Shield matches for six seasons in a row?

42 From which team did Alan Shearer move to Newcastle in 1996?

43 Can you name the former Arsenal, Manchester City and Sunderland striker who had a chant and song about him and his 'discopants'?

44 Did Chelsea finish 2nd, 4th or 14th in the 1993/94 season?

45 Of which Premier League club was Steve McLaren assistant manager before becoming manager of Middlesbrough?

46 Can you name two of the three Premier League teams that Luis Boa Morte has played for?

47 Which Premier League team won the 2001 Charity Shield: Arsenal, Newcastle United or Liverpool?

48 Which team was relegated in the 1993/94 season on 42 points, while Southampton and Ipswich Town remained safe on 43?

49 Which TV personality became Arsenal's all-time leading goal scorer in 1997 with 179 goals to his credit?

50 What was unusual about all four goals scored in the winter 2003 derby game between the two Manchester clubs?

⚽⚽ REGULAR SEASON QUIZ 2 ⚽⚽

1 Former Chelsea, Leeds United and Wimbledon player, Vinnie Jones, was once sent off in less than five seconds from the start of a game: true or false?

2 What is the system of games used to decide the third team to be promoted to a higher division including the Premier League called?

3 What is the name of the American goalkeeper signed by Manchester United in 2003?

4 West Ham United and which other club were involved in a nine-goal thriller during the 1999/2000 season – a game which West Ham won 5-4?

5 In the 2002/03 season, were a total of 37 penalties, own goals or headers scored in the Premier League?

6 Every year a race for the official mascots of Premier League and other teams is held at Huntingdon racecourse: true or false?

7 In which year did Mark Hughes formally retire as a player to concentrate on being the manager of the Welsh national team?

8 Which side recorded the Premier League's biggest victory, beating Ipswich 9-0?

9 Which Premier League club counts England Rugby Union captain, Martin Johnson, as a famous fan?

10 Charlton is the only Premier League club never to have played at the old Wembley Stadium: true or false?

11 In the 1992/1993 season, which team won both the FA Cup and the League Cup but came tenth in the Premier League?

12 Which team finished fourth from bottom in the 2001/02 season and was relegated from the Premier League the next season?

13 Steve Marlet's £11.5 million transfer to which club became its record signing?

14 Everton have never finished above Liverpool in the Premier League: true or false?

15 For what country does Arsenal's Kanu play international football?

16 Which former Premier League team did Harry Redknapp manage before Portsmouth?

17 Which European trophy did Arsenal win in 1994?

18 Which 2003/04 Premier League team has a female managing director?

19 Against which team did two Arsenal players both score hat-tricks during the 2002/03 season?

20 In the first three seasons of the Premier League, how many points was a win worth?

21 For which three clubs has Kevin Campbell scored hat-tricks?

22 If you were watching a match whilst sitting in the Steve Bull Stand, at which club's ground would you be?

23 Has Southampton been out of the Premier League once, twice or never since its formation?

24 Which Dutchman was a former European Player of the Year and has managed two Premier League clubs?

25 Of all the Premier League teams, past and present, which has the shortest name?

26 At what Premier League club was Andy Cole a player before moving to Blackburn Rovers?

27 Can you name the former England manager who was appointed to help Bryan Robson keep Middlesbrough in the Premier League?

28 Which team went without an away win in the Premier League for more than fifteen months during 1999 and 2000?

29 From which club did Glen Johnson join Chelsea in 2003?

30 How many teams averaged more than 50,000 spectators throughout the 2002/03 season?

31 How many of the three sides promoted for the 2003/04 season were making their Premier League debut?

32 Which European trophy did Chelsea win in 1998?

33 Lucas Radebe, Mark Fish and Shaun Bartlett are Premier League players who have played international football for which country?

34 Fratton Park is the home ground of which Premier League team?

35 Which two sixteen-year-olds scored Premier League goals in the 2002/2003 season against goalkeepers more than twice their age?

36 In 1993/94, which team scored more goals at home than any other team, yet finished fourth from bottom?

37 For what club did Les Ferdinand play when he scored 24 goals to come third in the 1994/95 season?

38 Which East London club was relegated in the 2002/03 season?

39 How many current or former Premier League clubs have the word 'valley' in their ground name?

40 Who won the 2003 League Cup?

41 How many away matches did Wimbledon win in the 1999/2000 season?

42 Which former centre half, nicknamed 'Stroller', managed Tottenham Hotspur after previously managing Arsenal?

43 What shape corner flags can football teams fly if they have won the FA Cup?

44 Which team scored eleven goals against Newcastle in its two 2002/03 Premier League games?

45 Were Chelsea, Arsenal or Southampton the first team to beat Manchester United in the 1999/00 season?

46 Who was awarded the Barclaycard Premiership Manager of the Year for 2002/03?

47 Which Premier League team played in the 2002/03 UEFA Cup after playing in the Inter Toto Cup the same season?

48 Which Yorkshire club made its first appearance in the Premier League in the 1997/1998 season?

49 Who qualified for a 2003 European Competition because of their high placing in the Premier League Fair Play table?

50 How many different current or former Premier League clubs has Ashley Ward scored goals for?

REGULAR SEASON QUIZ 3

1 How many Premier League medals did Bryan Robson win?

2 Can you name the three Premier League clubs Teddy Sheringham has played for in the past four years?

3 What team recorded its highest ever finish of second place in the very first season of the Premier League?

4 Which tempestuous Italian player was banned for eleven matches for pushing over a referee in the 1998/99 season?

5 Which former Premier League side plays at Bramall Lane?

6 Which Tottenham Hotspur player scored in his first full match for England in a 2004 friendly against Portugal?

7 Which Premier League team played at Anfield before Liverpool?

8 From which country does Manchester United's Diego Forlan come from?

9 If you arrange all the teams who have played in the Premier League in alphabetical order, who comes last?

10 Which Premier League player tragically died whilst playing an international game for Cameroon in the summer of 2003?

11 Which Italian footballer was Sheffield Wednesday's top scorer in the 1998/99 season?

12 Brian McBride played for Everton in the 2002/03 season. Was his former team: Hamilton Academicals, York City, Columbus Crew or Inter Milan?

13 Which former Premier League team plays at Carrow Road?

14 Which Leeds legend scored 24 goals in just 44 games during his three seasons with the club?

15 Olympian Denise Lewis, former Monty Python member Eric Idle and newsreader Sue Lawley are all fans of which Premier League team from the Midlands?

16 Which team, in 2003, managed their first league win away to Leeds for the first time in 37 attempts?

17 What is the name of the addiction treatment clinic that ex-Arsenal and England captain Tony Adams set up?

18 Which former Premier League club plays its matches at Hillsborough?

19 What is the name given to the man who displays the amount of injury time to be played in a Premier League game?

20 At the start of the 2003/04 season, who was the youngest manager of a Premier League team: Steve Bruce, Chris Coleman or Gordan Strachan?

21 In what year did Bobby Robson join Newcastle United as manager?

22 Chelsea replaced Glenn Hoddle as player-manager with another player-manager. Can you name him?

23 Which team won the 1995/96 Premier League title despite their leading scorer only netting fourteen goals?

24 Which famous England defender was Nottingham Forest player-manager for the 1996/97 season after he had memorably celebrated a successful penalty shootout against Spain in Euro 96?

25 By what bird nickname is the former Premier League club of Norwich City known?

26 Who made most Premier League appearances for Arsenal in the 2002/03 season: Sol Campbell, Thierry Henry or Ray Parlour?

27 Which Manchester United footballer failed to perform a drugs test in 2003?

28 Which Premier League club used to play its games at Maine Road?

29 Who won Manager of the Year in the Premier League for the 1994 season?

30 Everton and one other team won more away games than home games in the 1992/93 season. What was the other team?

31 Of the 22 Premier League teams in the 1993/94 season, how many were not in the 2003/04 Premier League: four, six, eight or ten?

32 Who scored the winning goal in the 1995/96 FA Cup Final to ensure Manchester United won a league and cup double?

33 At the start of 2004, how many clubs in the top five were from London?

34 Dougie Freedman, with nine goals, was which team's leading goal scorer of 1998/99?

35 Was Jason Euell Charlton Athletic's most expensive signing or biggest sale?

36 In the opening game of the 2001/02 season, who beat Leicester City 5-0?

37 During the 2002/03 season, who became the tenth player to score 100 Premier League goals?

38 Which former Premier League club, based in South London, is supported by comedians Jo Brand, Eddie Izzard, Sean Hughes and Ronnie Corbett?

39 Which Liverpool defender scored two own goals in a 1999 match against Manchester United?

40 Which team from the Midlands played its first ever Premier League games in 2003?

41 Which Coventry City striker was the joint leading Premier League goal scorer in the 1997/98 season?

42 Up to and including the 2002/03 season, which former Premier League player holds the joint record for the most appearances in the Champions League and European Cup?

43 In his first Premier League start for Arsenal,
    Jermaine Pennant scored a hat-trick. In the
    same game, who also scored three goals?

44 Which famous Scottish striker was
    manager of Blackburn Rovers in their
    first season in the Premier League?

45 How many former or current Premier
    League team names end with 'City'?

46 Against which side did Wolverhampton
    Wanderers record their first Premier
    League victory?

47 Who made most Premier League
    appearances for Tottenham Hotspur in the
    2002/2003 season: Robbie Keane, Kasey
    Keller or Stephen Carr?

48 What is the name of Aston Villa's stadium?

49 Which team did not win a single away
    game in the 1992/93 Premier League
    yet still finished three places above the
    relegation zone?

50 Which Premier League team won the
    European Super Cup in 2001?

1   Southampton won an amazing 1993/94 season match 5-4 against which team?

2   In 1999, who scored five goals in a Premier League match against Sheffield Wednesday?

3   Can you name the Premier League club Junichi Inamoto was with before he eventually arrived at Fulham?

4   Who managed West Bromwich Albion in their first season in the Premier League?

5   Which footballer won the PFA Young Player of the Year award in 2002?

6   How many seasons did Wimbledon manage to stay in the Premier League: three, five or eight?

7   Who was Arsenal's top scorer for six seasons in a row?

8   Which club made its Premier League debut in 2003 and because its game against Aston Villa was brought forward, played the very first match of the 2003/04 season?

9　Up to and including the 2003/04 season, how many teams have played in the Premier League: 31, 38, 45 or 52?

10　Did Nottingham Forest, Ipswich Town or Swindon lose 8-1 to Manchester United in the 1998/99 season?

11　Which Ipswich Town striker was runner-up as the 2000/01 season leading goal scorer?

12　West Ham United and which other London team shared a thrilling 4-4 draw in the 2001/02 season?

13　Which Premier League side from the Midlands are nicknamed 'the Villans'?

14　Which former Premier League club plays at Oakwell?

15　Which former player was Liverpool manager when the Premier League started?

16　Which Premier League team played its 2003/04 matches at Loftus Road, Queens Park Rangers' ground?

17 Which Premier League footballer won the PFA Young Player of the Year award in 2003?

18 Which Premier League team do England Rugby Union stars Matt Dawson and Austin Healey support: Leicester City, Everton or Arsenal?

19 Which former Newcastle United, Tottenham Hotspur and Everton star is famous for the tears he cried during a World Cup match?

20 Doug Ellis is the famous and long-serving chairman of which Premier League club?

21 Which two east of England rivals were both relegated in 1994/95?

22 In the first season of the Premier League, which team was relegated despite scoring 49 points?

23 Which Scottish team beat two Premier League sides in the 2002/03 UEFA Cup competition?

24 Which three Premier League sides has Peter Schmeichel played in goal for?

25 Who was Chelsea's leading Premier League goal scorer with eleven goals in the 1997/98 season?

26 How many penalties did Sunderland convert into goals in the 2002/03 season?

27 Which team did Dwight Yorke play for before he joined Manchester United?

28 Which Italian footballer who played for Middlesbrough and Derby County was nicknamed 'the white feather'?

29 In 2002, did Manchester City, Liverpool or Tottenham Hotspur spend the most money on buying players?

30 Which Irish winger did Blackburn Rovers sell for around £17 million in 2003?

31 For which London team did Sol Campbell make 255 appearances before moving to Arsenal?

32 Which Middlesbrough central defender has made more than 360 appearances in the Premier League: Ugo Ehiogu, Gareth Southgate or Colin Cooper?

33 Benito Carbone has scored goals for five Premier League clubs: can you name two of them?

34 Which Premier League club has the nickname 'the Toffees'?

35 Which Premier League team won the 1997 Charity Shield: Chelsea, Newcastle United or Manchester United?

36 How many teams relegated in the 1999/2000 season have since returned to the Premier League?

37 Which London-based club finished eleventh in three out of the first four seasons of the Premier League?

38 Which well-travelled manager is known as the 'Bald Eagle': Ron Atkinson, Joe Kinnear, Jim Smith or Bobby Gould?

39 Which former Premier League team are nicknamed 'the Superhoops'?

40 One Aston Villa player played in every single game of the 2002/03 Premier League season. Can you name him?

41 Who beat Manchester United 2-0 to win the 2000 Charity Shield?

42 Does Arsenal, Chelsea, Ipswich Town or Aston Villa hold the record for the most consecutive wins in one season?

43 Who was the leading scorer in the Premier League in the 2002/03 season?

44 Who was Everton's manager when the Premier League began: Walter Smith, Howard Kendall or Mike Walker?

45 From the start of the Premier League up to and including the 2002/03 season, how many times have Arsenal won the FA Cup?

46 Which former Premier League team's players were once known as the 'crazy gang'?

47 Which Premier League club had three managers in the 2002/03 season?

48 Who has managed Bolton Wanderers since October 1999?

49 Which Premier League player became the youngest England international when he debuted against Australia in 2003?

50 Which team did Newcastle United beat 6-1 in the 1995/96 season?

⚽⚽ REGULAR SEASON QUIZ 5 ⚽⚽

1 Who plays their football at the Stadium of Light?

2 Which Chelsea footballer played seven seasons in the Premier League, never received a red card, and in three seasons never received a yellow?

3 Middlesbrough have never lost a home Premier League fixture to which London side in all seven of their Premier League matches?

4 Which Premier League club supporters are famous for their chant of 'Boing, Boing'?

5 Which midfielder moved from Charlton to Leeds United for £2.6 million in 1996?

6 Which French footballing star in the Premier League advertised a make of car with the phrase, 'Va-Va-Voom'?

7 Which team won the Premier League and FA Cup in the 1997/98 season?

8 Dion Dublin was which team's leading Premier League goal scorer in 1998/99?

9 Who beat Nottingham Forest 7-0 in the 1995/96 season?

10 Is the record transfer fee paid for a player in the Premier League, £17 million, £21 million, £24 million or £30 million?

11 Which north-eastern Premier League team counts ex-MI5 spy David Shayler and singer-songwriter Chris Rea amongst its famous fans?

12 Which Merseyside team has been in the Premier League or the first division since 1954?

13 Which former Premier League club has a matchday mascot called Jude the Cat?

14 In the 1993/94 season which team won twice as many away games (eight) as they did home games?

15 Which Argentinean midfielder moved from Manchester United to Chelsea in 2003 for an estimated £17 million?

16 Which former Premier League team plays its football at Vicarage Road?

17 At the end of the 2002/03 season, two strikers were tied as the third highest all-time Premier League goal scorers? Can you name the ex-Liverpool player who later joined Manchester City?

18 Can you name any one of the three teams who beat Swindon Town 5-0 in their one season in the Premier League?

19 From which Premier League club did Japanese midfielder Junichi Inamoto go on loan to Fulham?

20 Which team holds the highest average attendance record for every Premier League season up to and including the 2002/03 season?

21 Ricardo was a Manchester United squad player in 2002/03, but was he a goalkeeper, a striker or a midfielder?

22 Which Premier League team counts snooker player Steve Davies, comedian Jim Davidson and Grandstand presenter Steve Ryder as famous fans?

23 Which fiery young Leeds striker holds the record for the best goal scoring performance by a Leeds player in Europe when he scored four goals in a 2002 game?

24 Which Dutch player with dreadlocks managed Chelsea in the late 1990s and bought Gianfranco Zola and Gianluca Vialli to the Premier League?

25 Who plays their football at the Riverside Stadium?

26 Which team has not lost at home to 24 of the total of 38 teams who have played in the Premier League?

27 Ivan Campo got more yellow cards in the Premier League in 2002/03 than any other player. How many cards was he given?

28 Which Premier League team won the 1995 Charity Shield: Tottenham Hotspur, Everton or Blackburn Rovers?

29 Which Manchester City striker made his Premier League debut as an Arsenal player?

30 When Ipswich was in the Premier League, what was the name of its home stadium?

31 Who finished second in the Premier League in its very first year?

32 Which team averaged more spectators per game in the 1993/94 season: Sheffield United or Chelsea?

33 Which former Leeds player became caretaker manager of the club in November 2003?

34 Oldham Athletic were members of the Premier League for its first two seasons: true or false?

35 Which famous striker is the father of Manchester City's Shaun Wright-Philips?

36 Which former England goalkeeper moved away from Arsenal on a free transfer in 2003?

37 West Bromwich Albion were originally called Bromwich Strollers: true or false?

38 Which England international Premier striker, who has played in the Premier League every season since it started, began his career as an apprentice at Millwall in 1984?

39 Defender Pat Rice is assistant manager at which Premier League club?

40 What was the name of Sunderland's former stadium?

41 Which retired Premier League star was famous for only missing one of 50 penalty kicks he took during his career?

42 Who was the second highest goal scorer in the Premier League's 2002/03 season?

43 Which team knocked Chelsea out of the FA Cup for the fourth time in 2004?

44 Who was the first English player to be involved in three transfers each worth a million pounds or more: Gary Lineker, Clive Allen or Ian Wright?

45 Hercules is the name of the official mascot of Charlton, Southampton or Aston Villa?

46 Of the four English League teams with the letter 'x' in their name, have one, two or no teams played in the Premier League?

47 For what Premier League club other than Arsenal had Nicolas Anelka played before joining Manchester City in 2002?

48 What is the most draws notched up in a Premier League by one team in a season: 12, 14, 18 or 22?

49 Which ex-Wimbledon, Chelsea and QPR hardman has made a career in movies such as Gone In 60 Seconds and Lock, Stock And Two Smoking Barrels?

50 For what country did Chelsea's Hernan Crespo appear and score, during the 2002 World Cup final?

REGULAR SEASON QUIZ 6

1 Which club let in the first ever Premier League goal?

2 What became the first club in the Nationwide league to be managed by former Arsenal and England captain, Tony Adams?

3 Which former Man United player won medals in both the Champions League and the European Championships?

4 Which Premier League team drew Yeovil Town in the 2003/04 FA Cup Third Round?

5 Who scored the winning goal in the 2003 FA Cup Final and for which club?

6 Southampton were beaten 7-1 in the 1996/97 season by: Everton, Sheffield Wednesday, Derby County or Coventry City?

7 Liverpool signed Steve Finnan from which other Premier League club for £3.5 million?

8 Who managed Leicester City during their 2003/04 Premier League campaign?

9 Manchester City have a striker who plays for Costa Rica in international competitions. Can you name him?

10 As a youngster, which famous player turned up to a trial for Tottenham Hotspur wearing a Manchester United shirt?

11 In 1998/99, which team finished fifth in the Premier League despite carding a -7 goal difference?

12 For which team do Gareth Barry and Lee Hendrie play?

13　In what season was there a change to the rules allowing players to score directly from the kick-off?

14　Dave Jones has managed two Premier League clubs. Can you name both of them?

15　Apart from Manchester City, what other club has Kevin Keegan managed in the Premier League?

16　Is Fred The Red, The Little Red Devil or Fergie The Fox the official mascot of Manchester United?

17　Which team lost 29 of their 38 games in the 1994/95 season, a Premier League record?

18　Emmanuel Petit has played for two London-based Premier League clubs. Can you name them both?

19　Which Premier League club has the nickname 'the Addicks': Birmingham City, Charlton Athletic or Fulham?

20 Which former Premier League team counts Billy Bragg, Nick Berry, Noel Edmonds and David Essex as fans?

21 What was the name of Middlesbrough's stadium prior to the Riverside?

22 Who first took over when Glenn Hoddle left Tottenham Hotspur as manager in 2003?

23 In the 1998/99 season, Manchester United and which other side suffered just three defeats?

24 Which Premier League team won the UEFA Cup in 2001?

25 Did Dave Bassett, Terry Burton or Joe Kinnear manage Wimbledon throughout the majority of their Premier League years?

26 Was Mark Crossley, Tim Flowers, David Seaman or David James the one goalkeeper to have saved a Matthew Le Tissier penalty?

27 Cilla Black, Mel C and Radio DJ John Peel are all supporters of which team?

28 Dion Dublin scored his 200th goal in all league and cup games in December, 2002. How many months earlier did he score his 100th Premier League goal?

29 In the 2003/04 season, Wolverhampton Wanderers had two players who had previously won the Premier League with which team?

30 Can you name either player?

31 Which tall Sunderland striker donated the money from his testimonial match to children's charities, raising over a million pounds in the process?

32 Can you name the Aston Villa, Manchester United and Blackburn Rovers striker who plays for Trinidad and Tobago?

33 Who was the Premier League's leading goal scorer for three seasons in a row?

34 From which club did Leeds sign Lee Bowyer?

35 Which side were on the receiving end of the worst Premier League thrashing?

36 In the first year of the Premier League, which team had the highest average attendance?

37 For which team did Frank Lampard play before joining Chelsea?

38 How many teams relegated in the 1995/96 season have since returned to the Premier League?

39 Which Premier League player became the youngest England international when he played against Australia in 2003?

40 Can you name one of the three teams who recorded the most draws in a Premier League season?

41 If you were walking down Sir Matt Busby Way, which football ground would you be approaching?

42 What was the name of Bolton Wanderers' ground prior to the Reebok Stadium?

43 How many Premier League teams has Ron Atkinson managed?

44 How many different teams have won the Premier League up to the 2002/03 season?

45 Did Blackburn Rovers win the 1994/95 Premier League by a one, three, five or nine point margin?

46 Up to the end of 2003, only one World Footballer of the Year has ever played in the Premier League. Can you name him?

47 And can you name either of the Premier League clubs he played for?

48 Which Premier League side holds the record for the largest victory in an FA Cup final?

49 And which former Premier League side did they beat?

50 Who was the leading Premier League goal scorer in the 1999/2000 season?

1   Steve McManaman played for which Premier League club before joining Real Madrid?

2   Who made a club record number of appearances for Arsenal before going on to become a Premier League manager for Leeds United?

3   Which Premier League club can count upon singer Craig David, athletics presenter Roger Black and Sir David Frost as supporters?

4   Which English player's two transfers within the Premier League totalled around £48 million?

5   Which former Manchester United player and assistant coach was in charge of Blackburn Rovers when they were relegated in the 1998/99 season?

6   Newcastle United inflicted Swindon Town's worst defeat of their one Premier League season. Was the score: 6-0, 7-1, 8-2 or 9-0?

7 In the first season of the Premier League, which team finished fifth and was London's highest-placed club?

8 In which season were four teams relegated instead of three to decrease the number of Premier League teams: 1994/95, 1997/98 or 1999/2000?

9 Who took the penalties for Everton in the 2002/03 season: Wayne Rooney, Kevin Campbell, Gary Naysmith or David Unsworth

10 Which club's supporters famously chant 'You'll never walk alone'?

11 Who was the first PFA Young Player of the Year winner not to be from Britain?

12 Ipswich has twice received £6 million for players; one a midfielder in 1999, the other a goalkeeper in 2002. Can you name either player?

13 Which former England manager resigned from managing Aston Villa in May 2003?

14 At the end of the 2002/03 season, two strikers were tied as the third highest all-time Premier League goal scorers? Can you name the ex-QPR, Newcastle and Tottenham Hotspur player?

15 In the first ten years of the Premier League what position was the worst finish for Manchester United?

16 Which Arsenal striker had more shots on target than any other Premier League player during 2002/03?

17 Which 2002/03 team collected more yellow cards than any other?

18 Who was voted player of the decade at the 2003 PFA Awards: Roy Keane, Alan Shearer, David Seaman or David Beckham?

19 Which former Premier League club joined the Football League in 1938: Wimbledon, Bradford City or Ipswich Town?

20 Which Welsh striker was West Ham United's leading goal scorer in the 1997/98 Premier League?

21 In the 1992/93 season Sheffield United beat Tottenham Hotspur 6-0: true or false?

22 What were referee's assistants known as in the early 1990s?

23 Which Irishman managed Leicester City between 1995 and 2000 before moving on to managing Celtic?

24 What nationality is Newcastle United's winger, Nolberto Solano?

25 Who made most Premier League appearances for Everton in the 2002/03 season: Kevin Campbell, Alan Stubbs or David Unsworth?

26 Which club's ground is the only one in the Premier League to feature a genuine old cottage amongst its stands?

27 Which Premier League side do TV presenters Ant and Dec, as well as Brendan Foster and actor Jimmy Nail, support?

28 Can you name all four men who managed Leeds United during the 2002/03 season?

29 Did Manchester City pay £7.5 million, £11 million, £13 million or £17.5 million for Nicolas Anelka?

30 What is the name of the match which traditionally starts the season featuring the winners of the Premier League versus the winners of the FA Cup?

31 How many places did QPR finish above Chelsea in the 1992/93 season?

32 Who thrashed Southampton 7-1 in the 1998/99 season?

33 Which former current or ex-Premier League club are nicknamed 'the Robins'?

34 How many pairs of Premier League teams have had the same first word in their names?

35 Which team only let in seventeen goals over the whole 1998/99 season, a Premier League record?

36 Which team holds the record for goals scored against them in the Premier League season?

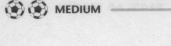
37 How many times have Manchester City finished above Manchester United in the Premier League: never, once, twice or three times?

38 Which Australian player scored fourteen goals for Leeds United in a ten-game period in 2002/03?

39 How many times have Bolton been relegated from the Premier League?

40 Who had played for six French clubs before joining Leeds United in 1992?

41 Which club was Arsène Wenger managing, the first time a side of his defeated Manchester United?

42 Which Premier League side from the North West of England are nicknamed 'the Trotters'?

43 Which premiership club did Dave Jones manage prior to Wolverhampton Wanderers?

44 What Premier League side are known as 'the Foxes'?

45 One Manchester City player played in every Premier League game of the 2002/03 season. Who was he?

46 Liverpool bought two players from which African nation that defeated France in the opening game of the 2002 World Cup?

47 In 2002/03, Fulham recorded the lowest Premier League attendance of the season with which visiting team: Everton, Southampton, Sunderland or Blackburn Rovers?

48 Which Premier League club did Brazilian World Cup 2002 winner, Roque Junior, play for during the 2002/03 season?

49 Did Chelsea or Liverpool average more spectators during the 2002/03 season?

50 In the 1999/2000 season, which team was thrashed 7-1 by Manchester United?

1   Who made most Premier League appearances for Chelsea in the 2002/03 season: Carlo Cudicini, Marcel Desailly or Frank Lampard?

2   Bradford City hold the record for the worst defeat in the Premier League, losing 11-0: true or false?

3   What nationality is David Moyes, the manager of Everton?

4   Which team finished third in 1992/93 only to be relegated two seasons later?

5   Who was Chelsea's leading Premier League scorer in 1998/99?

6   In what year did Graeme Souness join Blackburn Rangers as manager?

7   In which year did Bryan Robson start as manager of Middlesbrough?

8   If you were watching Kevin Campbell and Sean Davies in action at their home stadium of Goodison Park, which team would you be viewing?

9 Which famous horseracing jockey was, in 2003, chairman of Swindon Town?

10 What is the name of the son of a former England and Liverpool goalkeeper who now plays for Birmingham City?

11 Who was awarded the Barclaycard Premiership Player of the Year for 2002/03?

12 As of the start of the 2003/04 season, an Arsenal player holds the record for the fastest ever goal scored in the Champions League. Was it scored by Thierry Henry, Sylvain Wiltord or Gilberto Silva?

13 What former Premier League club's largest transfer windfall came when they sold Les Ferdinand to Newcastle United for £6 million?

14 Which Liverpool player won the PFA Young Player of the Year award in 2001?

15 Who scored 22 Premier League goals for Nottingham Forest in the 1994/95 season?

16 Who kept goal for the United States during the 2002 World Cup?

17 Who scored 25 1993/94 Premier League goals to become Norwich City's leading scorer?

18 Which popular player for Manchester City was the subject of a chant, 'Feed The Goat'?

19 Sheffield United lost all four of its Premier League games against only one side. Who was it?

20 Which former Manchester United and West Bromwich Albion midfielder captained England and was known by the nickname 'Captain Marvel'?

21 Which London-based Premier League's youth team did snooker champion Ronnie O'Sullivan play for as a child?

22 What is the name of the Premier League ground that contains a Clock End and a North Bank?

23 Which player scored more than half of all of Southampton's goals in the 2002/03 season?

24 Which team is the most northerly of all the clubs to have played in the Premier League?

25 Who spent more on transfers in the year 2002: Liverpool, Middlesbrough or Arsenal?

26 Which team used to play their football at Filbert Street?

27 Can you name the extremely tall Aston Villa player who made seven starts and seven appearances from the substitute's bench in 2002/03?

28 Which club signed goalkeeper Nigel Martyn, from Leeds, for the 2003/04 season?

29 How many of Andy Cole's 150 plus Premier League goals were penalties: 0, 12, 31 or 48?

30 How many yellow cards in a game automatically mean a sending off?

31 Who did Manchester United buy Roy Keane from?

32 Which football club plays at St Andrews stadium?

33 Who was the first foreign manager of the England national team?

34 What was the first season to see the Premier League start with only 20 teams in it?

35 Were over 30, 40, 50 or 60 different nationalities of player found in the 2002/03 Premier League?

36 Everton chairman Bill Kenwright is married to which actress: Jenny Agutter, Judi Dench or Penelope Keith?

37 Which Premier League team won the 2002 Charity Shield: Arsenal, Liverpool or Manchester United?

38 Did Liverpool receive their highest ever fee for the sale of Robbie Fowler, Jamie Redknapp or Steve McManaman?

39 The most money Bolton Wanderers have ever received for selling a player occurred back in 1995 with the sale of Jason McAteer to which other Premier League club?

40 What is the highest ever points total scored in the Premier League: 78, 83, 88 or 92?

41 Who was Arsenal's leading goal scorer in the 1996/97 season?

42 If you were watching Kieron Dyer, Jonathon Woodgate and Craig Bellamy from your seat in the Sir John Hall Stand, at which ground would you be?

43 Who was Manchester United's leading goal scorer of 1996/97: Andy Cole, Teddy Sheringham or Ole Gunnar Solskjaer?

44 Which team finished bottom of the 1996/97 Premier League?

45 How many Premier League teams made it through to the last sixteen of the 2003/04 Champions League?

46 If you were watching a team in claret shorts with sky blue sleeves sometimes nicknamed 'the Irons', would it be West Ham United, Barnsley or Aston Villa?

47 How many seasons have Watford played in the Premier League?

48 How many full England caps did Steve Bruce win?

49 Who was the manager of Everton before David Moyes?

50 Which Premier League team counts author Nick Hornby, the Appleton sisters from All Saints and TV presenter Clive Anderson as celebrity fans?

 **REGULAR SEASON QUIZ 9**

1 Which team scored the very first Premier League goal?

2　Which club received the most bookings in the 1999/2000 season?

3　What Premier League team counts cricketer, Nasser Hussein, Mel B and TV presenter, Jeremy Paxman as fans?

4　How many seasons have Everton finished above thirteenth place up to and including the 2002/03 season?

5　Sheffield Wednesday were at home to which club in 1994/95 when they were thrashed 7-1?

6　Who was the leading goal scorer of the entire Premier League in 1995/96 with 31 goals?

7　And how many of Newcastle United's 66 goals that season were not scored by Les Ferdinand or Alan Shearer: 10, 15, 20 or 25?

8　Who became Charlton's youngest ever player to make his first team debut in 1997, aged sixteen years and 93 days: Paul Konchesky, Scott Parker or Richard Rufus?

9 Which Premier League team had their first games in a European competition at the very start of the 2002/03 season?

10 Who was the manager of Liverpool immediately before Gerard Houllier?

11 Which former Premier League team were relegated a division after it was found they had made incorrect payments to players?

12 Can you name three of the five Premier League clubs that Wales Manager Mark Hughes played for?

13 Which Premier League star was the Champions League highest scorer in 2002/03?

14 Which team only one won away game in the 1994/95 Premier League?

15 Can you name the team that had the fewest number of clean sheets during the 2002/03 season?

16 Middlesbrough's Franck Queudrue was unfortunately top of what table of the Premier League 2002/03 season?

17 Which club is the most easterly of all the teams to have played in the Premier League?

18 Which Southampton footballer scored 23 Premier League goals during the 2002/03 season?

19 Did two, four, six or eight players score twenty or more Premier League goals in the 2002/03 season?

20 Who was the only Arsenal player to take a penalty besides Thierry Henry in the 2002/03 season?

21 What national team does Juan Sebastian Veron play for?

22 In 1999, Gary McSheffery became the youngest ever Premier League player when he appeared for: Coventry City, Bolton Wanderers or Southampton?

23 Which team scored a record 97 goals in one Premier League season: Newcastle United, Manchester United, Arsenal or Liverpool?

24 Which footballer has scored more penalties in the Premier League than any other?

25 Which team was the only one in the 1993/94 Premier League to not win a single away game?

26 What was the name of Southampton's ground before they moved to St Mary's?

27 If you were watching a team in royal blue shirts playing at home on Merseyside, which Premier League team would it be?

28 Which team averaged the fifth highest attendance in the 2002/03 season despite being relegated?

29 Chris Sutton was sold to which club in 1999 for around £10 million?

30 Only one of the three teams that finished on 38 points at the end of the 1995/96 season was relegated. Can you name it?

31 In what year was the first ever South Coast Derby in the Premier League, between Portsmouth and Southampton?

32 Which former Manchester United and Liverpool footballer is nicknamed 'the Guvnor'?

33 In August 2002, a former Italian defender's 81-day reign as Fulham's Director of Football ended. Who was he?

34 Can you name the striker who moved from Leeds to Athletico Madrid and then to Chelsea, both times involving transfer fees over £10 million?

35 David Dunn became which club's record signing when he moved for £5.5 million in 2003?

36 Which team scored just 21 goals in 38 games when they were relegated from the Premier League in 2003?

37 Which Premier League player was Japan's leading goal scorer of the 2002 World Cup?

38 Which Arsenal manager brought Dennis Bergkamp to the Premier League?

39 Which exciting Australian winger left Leeds to join Liverpool in 2003?

40 Manchester United beat two Yorkshire teams, 7-0 and 6-1, in the 1997/98 season. Can you name either team?

41 Jason Euell was which club's top scorer in the 2002/03 season?

42 Did Rio Ferdinand leave West Ham United, Leeds United or Tottenham Hotspur to go to Manchester United?

43 Which side beat Wolverhampton Wanderers 5-1 on the opening day of the 2003/04 season?

44 Was Joe Royle, Mick Wadsworth or Iain Dowie in charge of Oldham Athletic when they played in the Premier League?

45 How many Premier League teams past and present have single word names: four, six, twelve or eighteen?

46 From which city were the two biggest Premier League transfer spenders of 2002: London, Manchester or Birmingham?

47 Which team has Middlesbrough scored more goals against than any other, netting 26 times in just ten matches?

48 Which team holds the record for the least number of goals scored in a Premier League season?

49 Which Premier League club was once called Newton Heath?

50 From what country are Premier League players Fredrik Ljungberg, Matthias Svensson and Olof Mellberg?

⚽⚽ **REGULAR SEASON QUIZ 10** ⚽⚽

1 Which successful Premier League team is nicknamed 'the Red Devils'?

2 During the 2002/03 season, which Liverpool player became the youngest England international to reach 50 caps?

3 Which Premier League player was awarded the 2003 Player of the Year trophy?

4 Who scored Manchester United's first ever goal in the Premier League: Andy Cole, Steve Bruce, Mark Hughes or Roy Keane?

5 Which team, featuring Trevor Sinclair, Paulo Di Canio, David James and Joe Cole, was relegated in the 2002/03 season?

6 Which former Tottenham Hotspur manager was appointed England manager in 1994?

7 Referee Mike Riley awarded how many penalties for Manchester United in four League and Cup games at Old Trafford in 2002/03?

8 Which Manchester United player is known as the 'baby-faced assassin'?

9 Which Premier League club did Andy Cole begin his career with: Arsenal, Manchester United or Newcastle United?

10 Which footballer was just sixteen years old when he played for Everton versus Manchester United in 1997: Wayne Rooney, Danny Cadamarteri or Francis Jeffers?

11 Can you name the TV commentator who is affectionately known as 'Motty' to viewers?

12 Up to and including the 2002/03 season, can you name either of the teams which have been relegated from the Premier League a record three times?

13 Which team managed to do the triple of winning the Premier League, FA Cup and Champions League in 1998/99?

14 Which Liverpool player's wife is Sheree Murphy, former Emmerdale soap star?

15 'The Black Cats' is a nickname for which team: Middlesbrough, Leicester City, Sunderland or Oldham Athletic?

16 Tottenham Hotspur fans endured their worst home defeat of 1997/98, when which side beat them 6-1?

17 Which 2002/03 team used 34 players, the most by any side that season?

18 Which former Premier League team's ground is called Boundary Park?

19 Can you name either of the Leeds United players sent off in a stormy match against Arsenal in 2001?

20 Which former Premier League team is nicknamed 'the Rams'?

21 Which club did Wayne Bridge leave to join Chelsea in 2003?

22 Les Ferdinand and Rio Ferdinand are cousins: true or false?

23 Who ended the 2002/03 season as the goalkeeper with the most appearances in the Premier League but started the 2003/04 season outside of the Premier League?

24 Who was Manchester United's second leading scorer in the 2002/03 season: Paul Scholes, David Beckham or Ryan Giggs?

25 Which League Cup Final was the first to be won on penalties: 2000, 2001 or 2002?

26 Which Scotsman succeeded Walter Smith as manager of Everton?

27 On 23 September 2002, did Ryan Giggs, David Beckham or Andy Cole score his 100th goal for Manchester United?

28 How many times have Liverpool finished first or second in the Premier League?

29 Can you name two of the Premier League clubs American goalkeeper Brad Friedel has played for?

30 Which former Premier League club has the nickname 'the Owls'?

31 At which Premier League club did Michael Owen start his career?

32 Queen Elizabeth II opened the Dr Martens Stand at which Premier League club as part of her 2002 Golden Jubilee celebrations?

33 Which central defender moved from Tottenham Hotspur to arch rivals Arsenal in July 2001?

34 If you arranged all the teams who have played in the Premier League in alphabetical order, which team would appear at the very start of the list?

35 Former Middlesbrough and Leeds United defender, Paul Okon's first football club was in Australia. Was it called Marconi Stallions, Waratah Rangers or Sydney Athletic?

36 Against which team has Arsenal lost eleven and only won five of its 23 Premier League matches?

37 Which Welsh winger owns the most Premier League winner's medals of any player?

38 Can you name any one of the three players who finished as runners up in the 2001/02 leading Premier League scorers with 23 goals?

39 Which Manchester United midfielder fell out with the Republic of Ireland manager, Mick McCarthy and did not play at the 2002 World Cup Finals?

40 Did Wayne Bridge, Gary Neville or Ray Parlour create a Premier League record by playing 112 matches without being substituted?

41 Two teams with 'City' in their names were relegated in 1994/95. Can you name either of them?

42 Which famous Derby and Nottingham Forest manager retired from football during the first Premier League season?

43 Which 2003/04 Premier League team won the League Cup in 2000?

44 Manchester United averaged over 65,000 spectators per game in 2003. Did they average 35,500, 42,500, 49,500 or 54,500 in the first season of the Premier League?

45 Where did Manchester United finish in the 2001/02 season?

46 Hamilton Ricard scored fifteen Premier League goals in the 1998/99 season making him which club's leading scorer?

47 What is Leeds United's best finish in the Premier League?

48 Who was the chairman of Leeds in their best ever Premier League season?

49 Manchester United youngster, Darren Fletcher, plays his international football for which country?

50 Which team's nickname is 'the Cockerels': Tottenham Hotspur, Bradford City or Sheffield United?

REGULAR SEASON QUIZ 11

1 The 1995/96 and 1996/97 seasons both featured the same teams in first and second place. Who were they?

2 Who is the second longest serving manager in the Premier League, having joined the club in 1991?

3 In which season did all three teams to be relegated have the word 'City' in their name?

4 In 1997, the Charity Shield game was drawn 1-1. Did the teams share the trophy, toss a coin for it or play a penalty shootout?

5 Billy Bantam is the mascot of which former Premier League team?

6 Radio DJ Simon Mayo, and actors Jude Law and Kenneth Branagh, are supporters of which Premier League side?

7 Who finished bottom of the very first Premier League?

8 How many Premier League goals did Wayne Rooney score in the 2002/03 season?

9 Who holds the record for the least points scored in the Premier League?

10 Who scored the only goal in Wolves' first Premier League win: Paul Ince, Colin Cameron or Denis Irwin?

11 Which Southampton footballer scored an incredible 209 league and cup goals in 462 games for the side?

12 In the 2002/03 season, can you name the only Premier League club with an average attendance of below 20,000?

13 In what year did Kevin Keegan join Manchester City as manager?

14 Can you name either of the Premier League-winning goalkeepers employed by Manchester City in the 2002/03 or 2003/04 seasons?

15 Who beat Newcastle United 5-0 in November 2003, in the Premier League?

16 Which two Manchester United assistant managers have gone on to manage Premier League clubs?

17 Which Arsenal midfielder was banned for three games for pushing referee Paul Durkin, in 1997?

18 Which player came on as a substitute for Manchester United and proceeded to score four goals in an 8-1 victory in 1998/99?

19 Which two former Premier League clubs has Paul Jewell managed?

20 For which Premier League side did Juergen Klinsmann play?

21   Which Newcastle United player was substituted a record 22 times during the 2002/03 season?

22   Which football team has the nickname 'the Hornets'?

23   Which much-travelled Premier League player's list of clubs includes: Charlton, West Ham, Sheffield Wednesday, Celtic, Milan, Juventus, Napoli and Lazio?

24   Which Premier League team was formed in 1919 and included among its great players Peter Lorimar, Harry Kewell and Eric Cantona?

25   Which team gave away three own goals to Charlton Athletic in February 2003?

26   Which Premier League club competing in the 2003/04 season is known as 'the Cottagers'?

27   Which former Gillingham, Norwich and Manchester United defender managed Birmingham City when they joined the Premier League in 2002/2003?

28 In November 2003 which team beat Leeds United, 6-1: Arsenal, Portsmouth or Chelsea?

29 What team took 45 points from a possible 51 from the end of 2002 to May 2003?

30 What was unusual about the Chelsea team that faced Coventry City on 15 August 1998?

31 Which Arsenal midfielder was sent off twice in three days during the 2000/01 season?

32 What is the name of Bolton Wanderers' stadium: the Reebok, Pride Park or the Riverside?

33 What was unusual about Julian Dicks being West Ham's joint leading goal scorer in the 1995/96 season?

34 Who was the chairman of Wolves when they played in the Premier League for the first time?

35 Which Premier League team conceded a record 100 goals in the 1993/94 season?

36 Which famous football pundit said, 'You can't win the league with kids' on television after a young Manchester United side were well beaten?

37 Who was the first Premier League manager to be removed from office in the 2003/04 season?

38 Which former assistant to Alex Ferguson became manager of Middlesbrough in 2001?

39 For which team was Dean Holdsworth playing when he finished third highest goal scorer of the 1992/93 Premier League?

40 Which football team plays its football at Upton Park?

41 Which Premier League club did eccentric goalkeeper Bruce Grobbelaar eventually move to after a long, successful spell at Liverpool?

42 How many Premier League championship medals did Steve Bruce win with Manchester United?

43 Which Premier League club is sometimes described as the 'School of Science'?

44 Which Manchester United midfielder put in a transfer request in January 2004?

45 Which Leeds midfielder had a short spell with West Ham United in their relegation season before signing for Newcastle United?

46 Who was the first Premier League manager to be sacked during the 2002/03 season?

47 Manchester United bought a striker for over £12 million and sold him a few seasons later to Blackburn Rovers for around £2 million. Who was he?

48 Which TV celebrity and former striker for Tottenham Hotspur, Leicester City and Everton, was part of the bid to rescue Leicester from financial ruin in 2002?

49 Against which south London football team did David Beckham score a sensational goal from inside his own half?

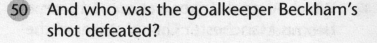

50 And who was the goalkeeper Beckham's shot defeated?

REGULAR SEASON QUIZ 12

1 The County Ground is the home of a team who had just one Premier League season. Can you name them?

2 Manchester City's new stadium was first used to hold which international sporting event?

3 Which Premier League team has the most letters in its name?

4 Which former Premier League club counts celebrity cook Delia Smith as one of its directors?

5 Who did Manchester United beat in the final to win the 1999 Champions League?

6 Which Liverpool striker won the PFA Young Player of the Year in both 1995 and 1996?

7 Which Arsenal striker was named after a famous Manchester United striker of the past?

8 Who has scored goals for Tottenham Hotspur, Middlesbrough, Liverpool, Everton and Leeds United?

9 Which French striker scored in a Merseyside Derby and a Manchester Derby both in the same year, 2002?

10 Between 1999 and 2001 which club used nine different goalkeepers, including an Australian, a Dutchman, a Frenchman and an Italian?

11 Which former Premier League club has the nickname 'the Tykes'?

12 Which football team's ground is called Molineux: Sheffield Wednesday, Wolverhampton Wanderers or Fulham?

13 Until Ruud van Nistelrooy arrived, Mark Stein held the record for scoring in seven Premier League games in a row. Was he playing for Sunderland, Middlesbrough, Chelsea or Southampton at the time?

14 Which team lost fifteen games in a row during the 2002/03 season, a Premier League record?

15 Which team won the very last First Division title before it was transformed into the Premier League?

16 Before the 2003/04 season, when was the last season that a single player scored 30 or more Premier League goals?

17 Newcastle United signed the first Colombian player to play in the Premier League. What was his name?

18 Up to and including the 2002/03 season, how many times have Manchester United won the Premier League?

19 Which team with the word 'Athletic' in its name was relegated from the Premier League in the 1993/94 season?

20 Which former Manchester United player is the son of Dutch football legend, Johan Cruyff?

21 Which former Premier League club has shared its stadium with Wasps rugby union club and Fulham football club?

22 What nationality was Liverpool and Tottenham Hotspur striker Ronnie Rosenthal?

23 Bradford City and which other former Premier League club shared eight goals in a thrilling 1999/2000 match?

24 Did Oldham Athletic have one, two or three seasons in the Premier League?

25 Which Midlands club did the England defender Matthew Upson join in 2003?

26 Sunderland's leading goalscorer in 2002/03 was Kevin Phillips, but did he score 6, 9 or 13 goals?

27 Can you name either of the Premier League clubs that winger Keith Gillespie was at prior to moving to Leicester City?

28 Which Premier League club is nicknamed 'the Magpies'?

29 The Governor of the Bank of England, Eddie George, and Liam and Noel Gallagher from Oasis are supporters of which Premier League club?

30 For what Premier League team was David Batty playing when he was banned for six games for pushing referee, David Elleray?

31 Manchester United, Arsenal and which other Premier League club entered the 2000/01 Champions League?

32 In the 1999/2000 season, which team were thrashed 7-2 by Tottenham Hotspur?

33 Which ex-Premier League manager and well-known TV pundit is nicknamed 'Big Ron'?

34 Which team's stadium is sometimes described as the 'Theatre of Dreams'?

35 Which manager of Wales has scored goals for five different Premier League clubs?

36 Which former Everton striker rejoined his old club in 2003 after two unfruitful seasons at Arsenal?

37 What is the record number of goals scored by a single player in a Premier League match?

38 Who made most Premier League appearances for Manchester United in the 2002/03 season: Mikael Silvestre, Ryan Giggs or Paul Scholes?

39 Laurence Dallaglio, Sebastian Coe and Sir Richard Attenborough are all fans of which London-based Premier League club?

40 Players from which Premier League team won the PFA Young Player of the Year award in both 2002 and 2003?

41 Teddy Sheringham was playing for which team when he finished the 1992/93 season as leading goal scorer?

42 Can you name either of Arsenal's permanent managers before Arsène Wenger during the time of the Premier League?

43 Up until the summer of 2003, the most Fulham has ever made on a transfer was £800,000 for Tony Thorpe: true or false?

44 Who finished third in the Premier League in the 2002/03 season?

45 Andy Cole and Alan Shearer finished the 1993/94 season as the two leading goal scorers. Which one played for Newcastle United?

46 Which Welsh striker was the last Wimbledon player to score a goal in the Premier League for the club?

47 Who was the first Premier League player to break the English transfer record when he moved from Manchester United to Inter Milan in 1995?

48 Who won Manager of the Year in the Premier League for the 1994/95 season?

49 Manchester United brothers, Gary and Phil Neville's father is called Neville Neville: true or false?

50 At which Premier League side's ground did David Beckham make his last appearance for Manchester United?

1   How many Premier League managers have Manchester United had, up to and including the 2003/04 season?

2   Can you name the Chelsea striker in the 2002/03 season who plays international football for Iceland?

3   In 1996/97, which team had three points deducted for failing to fulfil a Premier League fixture and were relegated by just two points?

4   Wimbledon's biggest league win in the 1999/2000 season was a 5-0 victory over which side?

5   Which Leeds United footballer gave away more fouls than any other 2002/03 Premier League player?

6   Which Premier League side in the past was one of the last to install floodlights, only fitting them to their ground in 1962?

7   Leicester City and Tottenham Hotspur goalkeeper Ian Walker's father was a Premier League manager. Can you name either of the sides he managed?

8 Which Premier League team have Liverpool beaten more times than any other (14 wins out of 23 games)?

9 Which Chelsea and England midfielder's father has the same name and was a long-serving defender with West Ham?

10 Which team scored a whopping 53 goals in just 19 games at home during the 1996/97 season?

11 Up to the end of the 2002/03 season, which player had made the most Premier League appearances: David Beckham, Teddy Sheringham, Gary Speed or David Seaman?

12 In 1995, Arsenal broke the national transfer record when they signed which Dutch player?

13 How many 2003/04 Premier League clubs have their names starting and ending with the same letter?

14 Who was the Premier League's leading goal scorer for the 2000/01 season?

15 Jimmy Floyd Hasselbaink shared the leading 1998/99 scorer title with two other players. Can you name either of them?

16 What was the name of the only Frenchman to start the first round of games of the first season of the Premier League?

17 Which former Premier League club has a mascot called Rockin' Robin?

18 Which football team averaged 51,920 supporters at every Premier League match during the 2002/03 season?

19 Which team won the 1998 Charity Shield, beating Manchester United 3-0?

20 Which side thrashed Tottenham Hotspur 7-1 in 1996/97?

21 At what stadium were the 2002/03 season Play Off finals held?

22 Did Charlton first appear in the Premier League in the 1998/99, 1999/2000 or 2000/01 season?

23 Who was Leeds United manager when the Premier League started?

24 Which Premier League team's home strip features a red shirt with white sleeves?

25 For which country did Damien Duff, then a Blackburn player, perform well in the 2002 World Cup?

26 In the 2001/02 season which Manchester United winger came on as a substitute against Aston Villa and was then substituted himself later in the game?

27 Chaddy the Owl is the official mascot of which former Premier League club?

28 Which coach left Manchester United to manage Real Madrid?

29 Did Matt Le Tissier, Paul Gascoigne, David Beckham or Jamie Redknapp open his own nightclub, called Celebration Plaza?

30 Of the 2003/04 Premier League teams, which has been playing at its ground the longest (since 1888): Charlton, Chelsea or Wolverhampton Wanderers?

31 How many teams have never been relegated from the Premier League?

32 Derby County's youngest ever player debuted in 2002 and was under 16 years of age: true or false?

33 Which Manchester United player won Match of the Day's Goal Of The Season award for his mazy run and shot against Arsenal in 1999?

34 Which team has the nickname 'the Baggies'?

35 How many goals must a player score in a game to have a 'brace'?

36 Can you put these Leeds United Managers in order: Terry Venables, George Graham, Peter Reid, David O'Leary?

37 A 1994/95 Midlands Derby game ended with the two sides sharing eight goals between them. Can you name either team?

38 Who was the only team to beat Manchester United in the 1994/95 Premier League season at Old Trafford?

39 Which Premier League star was the Champions League highest scorer in 2001/02?

40 Who made most Premier League appearances for Liverpool in the 2002/03 season: Danny Murphy, Michael Owen or Emile Heskey?

41 Who took over managing West Ham for a short period after Glenn Roeder was ill in 2003?

42 Southampton sensationally beat which team 6-3 during the 1996/97 season?

43 Only one English Premier League footballer has won the European Footballer of the Year award. Can you name him?

44 Ruud van Nistelrooy scored six, eight, twelve or fourteen penalties in the 2002/03 Premier League?

45 One Newcastle United player played in every single game in the 2002/03 Premier League season. Can you name him?

46 Which Premier League club play their football at Ewood Park?

47 Can you name either of the London Premier League clubs Paolo Di Canio has played for?

48 Which team lost 14 out of 19 of their first 1999/2000 Premier League games?

49 Who was the first black referee to be appointed to the Premier League list?

50 Against whom were Manchester United three down at half time in a 2001 Premier League fixture only to win the match 5-3?

REGULAR SEASON QUIZ 14

1 Which of the following players did Liverpool pay the most for: Paul Ince, Stan Collymore or Patrik Berger?

2 Which team finished bottom of the 1996/97 good behaviour league after notching up 5 red cards and 83 yellow cards?

3   Which Norwegian striker scored for Manchester United on his debut in 1996?

4   And five years later, who was the next Manchester United player to score on his debut?

5   Which team had the lowest average attendance in the 1995/96 Premier League: Southampton, Derby County or Wimbledon?

6   Of which former Premier League club did Peter Ridsdale become chairman after leaving Leeds United?

7   Can you name either of the clubs former England captain Gerry Francis has managed in the Premier League?

8   In the 2001/02 season, Manchester United's first defeat at home by three or more goals since 1992 occurred. Who won the game?

9   Against which Premier League team did Wolves register their first ever Premier League victory?

10 Which Sunderland player scored 38% of his team's 2001/02 Premier League goals?

11 Which player scored his 100th home Premier League goal for Newcastle United in December 2003?

12 Which Premier League star scored both goals in Liverpool's 2-1 FA Cup victory over Arsenal?

13 In which month of the year do Premier League teams first play in the FA Cup?

14 Did Chelsea beat West Bromwich Albion, Middlesbrough or Aston Villa to win the 1997 FA Cup?

15 Is the penalty spot 9m, 11m, 13m or 15m away from the goal line?

16 Which former Leeds and England manager co-wrote a detective series and the book, They Used To Play On Grass?

17 Which one of the following is not a French player at Fulham: Steed Malbranque, Luis Boa Morte or Alain Goma?

18 Which Premier League team's defenders in the 2003/04 season included players from Ecuador, Trinidad, Sweden, Ireland and Norway?

19 Which former Manchester United defender made over 510 appearances for the club from the early 1990s onwards?

20 Which of the following is not a French player at Arsenal: Patrick Viera, Kanu, Thierry Henry, Robert Pires?

21 For which country did Portsmouth and former Liverpool star, Patrik Berger play international football?

22 Who finished third in the 1994/95 season: Chelsea, Nottingham Forest, Liverpool or Everton?

23 In the 1997/98 season, which team suffered a 6-0 home defeat and a 7-0 away thrashing?

24 Which former Arsenal winger has also played for Middlesbrough, Portsmouth and Aston Villa?

25 Liverpool record goal scorer Ian Rush left the club in 1996 to join which other Premier League side?

26 Was Les Ferdinand, Alan Shearer or Eric Cantona the 1996 PFA Player of the Year?

27 Can you name either of the teams who tied for the most red cards in the 2001/02 season?

28 Which one of these three Liverpool legends did not join the club from Watford: John Barnes, John Aldridge or David James?

29 Which relegated Premier League team started the 2000/01 season in Division One with their goalkeeper sent off after just thirteen seconds?

30 Was the goalkeeper Raimond van der Gouw, Kevin Pressman, Fraser Digby or Thomas Sorenson?

31 Robbie Savage was at which Premier League club before his move to Birmingham City?

32 Milan Baros is from the Czech Republic, Bulgaria, Germany or Finland?

33 If a referee holds both his arms out in front of him when a foul is committed, is he signalling for a penalty, a free kick or to play advantage?

34 For which Premier League team did the Turkish defender, Tugay, play for?

35 For which Premier League team did World Cup winner, Didier Deschamps play?

36 What is the name given to the Italian equivalent of the Premier League?

37 Which striker joined Coventry City from Manchester United for £2 million in 1994?

38 Goalkeeper Craig Forrest plays international football for what country?

39 How many metres must a wall be away from a player taking a free kick: 7m, 9m, 12m or 15m?

40 At the start of 2004, who is the oldest manager of a Premier League team?

41 And what birthday did he celebrate in 2004?

42 Kevin Davies was at which Premier League club before he moved to Bolton Wanderers?

43 Manchester United beat Newcastle United 6-2 in the 2002/03 season but who scored a hat-trick during that game?

44 Who was Chelsea's first Premier League manager: Ian Porterfield, Glenn Hoddle or Gianluca Vialli?

45 Which Premier League team's ground is found on Floyd Road, London?

46 Roy McFarland was in charge of which club on their first season in the Premier League?

47 How many seasons were Blackburn Rovers in the Premiership before they were relegated?

48 The Teddy and Toddy strike partnership at Portsmouth featured Svetoslav Todorov and which former England forward?

49 With which team did young strikers Shola Ameobi and Lomana Tresor Lua Lua first play Premier League football?

50 Who was Birmingham City manager between 1996 and 2001 before Steve Bruce took over?

⚽⚽ **REGULAR SEASON QUIZ 15** ⚽⚽

1 Which Premier League team did Graeme Souness manage in 1996/97?

2 Tottenham Hotspur had two non-British managers during the 1990s. Can you name either of them?

3 If a referee's assistant points his flag to the front edge of the six-yard box what is he or she signalling for?

4 Which goalkeeper replaced David Seaman at Arsenal?

5 At the start of 2004 which Premier League striker had scored 97 goals in just 118 games?

6 For what country does striker Tomasz Radzinski play his international football?

7 Who was the Aston Villa manager before Graham Taylor: Steve McClaren, Peter Reid, John Gregory or Micky Evans?

8 In the summer of which year did Ruud van Nistelrooy join Manchester United?

9 Which London club surprisingly beat Chelsea 4-2 on Boxing Day, 2003?

10 If you had a seat for the game in the Jimmy Seed Stand would you be watching a Premier League match at Portsmouth, Southampton or Charlton Athletic?

11 Which member of the Arsenal defence plays international football for the Ivory Coast: Kolo Toure, Pascal Cygan or Lauren?

12 Juan Pablo Angel plays international football for which country?

13 At the very start of 2004, which London club was in the bottom three of the Premier League?

14 Which Premier League team is the only one to have a Professor, Professor John McKenzie, as a Chairman?

15 Which Premier League goalkeeper has a degree in mechanical engineering?

16 Which Premier League team's highest ever finish was seventh place back in 1994/95?

17 Which Tottenham Hotspur player was the only one to play every game of the 2002/03 season?

18 What is the name given to the German equivalent of the Premier League?

19 Which former Wolves, Coventry City, Leeds United and Inter Milan striker was signed by Tottenham Hotspur in 2002?

20 In January 2004, Kenny Miller scored the only goal as the bottom team in the Premier League beat the top team. Can you name the bottom side?

21 Who was the first Premier League team to win both the FA Cup and League Cup in the same season?

22 Which Sunderland and Derby County goalkeeper comes from Estonia?

23 Which Blackburn Rovers striker took just 65 games to score 50 goals: Andy Cole, Matt Jansen or Peter Beardsley?

24 In 2003/04, Newcastle United took Carlton Cole on a season's loan from which other Premier League team?

25 How many FA Cup finalists have come from Divisions One, Two or Three since the Premier League was formed?

26 How many teams with the word 'City' in their name were present in the very first season of the Premier League?

27 Can you name them?

28 In October 2001, Manchester United took the lead in a Premier League game only to lose the match. Was it the first, second or third time this had happened since the start of the Premier League?

29 Which team lost 26 of their 38 1999/2000 season games?

30 Which former Premier League team shared grounds with Wimbledon for a number of seasons?

31 Which team lost more games than any other in 2001/02, although they did not finish bottom?

32 Who finished highest in the 1992/93 Premier League: Chelsea, Liverpool, Queens Park Rangers or Arsenal?

33 If a referee sticks an arm straight up in the air, is he signalling for a direct free kick, an indirect free kick or a penalty?

34 Can a player be offside if they receive the ball directly from a throw-in?

35 Did Chelsea sign Ruud Gullit in 1995 from Sampadoria for £5.5 million, £3.75 million, £2.25 million or on a free transfer?

36 Premier League clubs first compete in which round of the FA Cup?

37 Which club did David Ginola join from Tottenham Hotspur for £3 million?

38 Chelsea's leading goal scorer in their first Premier League season scored nine goals. Was it Mick Harford, Paul Furlong, John Spencer or Mark Stein?

39 Which Manchester United defender was David Beckham's Best Man at his wedding?

40 In the first five Premier League seasons, how many times was Teddy Sheringham Tottenham Hotspur's leading goalscorer?

41 Who in 2001/02 scored 31% of his team's entire total of Premier League goals?

42 In 2002 did Karen Brady became the first female referee, managing director or coach of a Premier League club?

43 Which striker and now manager, enjoyed thirteen seasons at Manchester United before joining Chelsea?

44 Which of the following 'United' teams finished highest in the 1998/99 season: Newcastle United, West Ham United, Leeds United?

45 What name is given to the move where the ball is kicked through an opponent's legs?

46 The 1994/95 season saw an experiment with penalty shootouts deciding drawn Premier League games: true or false?

47 From which lower division club did Tottenham Hotspur sign Bobby Zamora?

48 Was Danny Mills, Paul Ince or Patrick Viera the most-booked player of the 2001/02 season?

49 Which team went 114 Premier League games between 1999 and 2002 without registering a goalless draw?

50 Which team lost 15 of their 38 games yet finished fourth in the 1997/98 season?

⚽⚽ **REGULAR SEASON QUIZ 16** ⚽⚽

1 Which team drew only three games in the 1997/98 season: Crystal Palace, Chelsea, Leicester City or Sheffield Wednesday?

2 For which country does Craig Bellamy play his international football?

3 Which Southampton player's first name is Marian?

4 Only one team managed to stay undefeated away from home throughout the 2001/02 season. Which team was it?

5 Which Costa Rican striker has played for Derby County, West Ham United and Manchester City?

6 What was the name of the hoaxer who appeared in a Manchester United official team photo before a 2001 Champions League game?

7 Which Premier League team has Darius Vassell played for since 1998/99?

8 Must both, one or neither foot be touching the ground when the ball is released in a throw-in?

9 Harpal Singh is a member of which Premier League team's squad?

10 By what name is Arsenal midfielder, Eduardo Cesar Daude Gaspar better known?

11 Which of the following is not a French player at Manchester City, Nicolas Anelka, Sylvain Distain, David Sommeil or Michael Tarnat?

12 In which season did Manchester United score 49 goals in its 19 Premier League home games?

13 Twelve teams formed the original football league. How many of those teams were in the 2003/04 Premier League?

14 If you were at the Railway End watching home players David Dunn and Christophe Dugarry in 2003/04, at which football ground would you be?

15 Defender Henning Berg has played for which club both before and after his time at Manchester United?

16 Was Stuart Gray, Graeme Souness or Glenn Hoddle in charge of Southampton before Gordon Strachan took over?

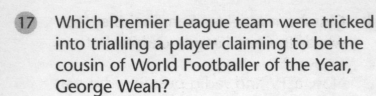

17 Which Premier League team were tricked into trialling a player claiming to be the cousin of World Footballer of the Year, George Weah?

18 Can you name either of the two teams which beat Norwich City in five out of their six Premier League matches?

19 For which Premier League club did the Ghanaian born striker, Elvis Hammond, sign a new contract in 2003?

20 Which Premier League team sold Andy Cole to Bristol City for just £500,000?

21 From what country are Premier League players Quinton Fortune, Lucas Radebe and Shaun Bartlett?

22 How many teams relegated in the 1997/98 season have since returned to the Premier League?

23 Which one of the following players was not a Manchester United player as a teenager: Jonathon Greening, Robbie Savage, Dwight Yorke, Mark Bosnich?

24 Chinese midfielder Sun Jihai plays for which Premier League club?

25 Now a TV and radio pundit, who was Sheffield Wednesday's leading goal scorer in their first two Premier League seasons?

26 The 2001 Charity Shield game won by Liverpool was the first major British match: to be played on artificial turf, to see five sendings-off, to be played indoors or to see three hat-tricks scored in the same game?

27 Which team did Chelsea's leading 2001/02 goalscorer, Jimmy Floyd Hasselbaink score five goals against in two games?

28 Which Premier League club spent an estimated £15 million on two Senegalese footballers?

29 Carrow Road is the home of which former Premier League club?

30 Which football club will in the next few years move to a new stadium in Ashburton Grove?

31 Which former Premier League team averaged the biggest attendances in Division Two in the first half of the 2003/04 season?

32 Can you name the side which beat Manchester United at Old Trafford in 2003 with goals from Kevin Nolan and Michael Ricketts?

33 Who won the BBC Sports Personality of the Year award in 1998?

34 Which one of the following was not a founder member of the football league: Bolton Wanderers, Manchester United, Everton?

35 Which Manchester City striker scored a last minute winner for Liverpool when they beat Newcastle United 4-3 in a thrilling encounter in 1997?

36 In October 1996, Manchester United scored three goals against Southampton but how many goals did Southampton score?

37 Which striker has been sold twice for £6 million and has played for QPR, West Ham, Newcastle and Tottenham Hotspur in the Premier League?

38 Which of the following players did Arsenal pay the most for: Patrick Viera, Marc Overmars or Dennis Bergkamp?

39 Brian Deane scored a fifth of all of Leicester City's 2001/02 Premier League goals. How many did he score?

40 How many seasons in a row was Alan Shearer Blackburn Rovers' top scorer?

41 Can you name two of the three players who scored two goals each in Newcastle United's 7-1 demolition of Tottenham Hotspur in 1996?

42 Up to and including the 2003/04 season, how many Premier League clubs have come from Yorkshire?

43 Which Premier League manager left his club in February 2004?

44 Which Israeli midfielder played previously for West Ham and Manchester City before moving to Portsmouth in 2004?

45 Who became the most expensive English teenager following a £5 million move from Nottingham Forest to Newcastle United?

46 And what was the name of the Portuguese winger who became the most expensive teenager in the Premier League in 2003?

47 Luis Boa Morte has played for three different Premier League clubs: can you name two of them?

48 If you were sitting in the Holte End would you be at Aston Villa, Tottenham Hotspur or Birmingham City's ground?

49 Can you name three of the five current or former Premier League teams Stan Collymore has played for?

50 Which goalkeeper became Manchester United's oldest player since 1921 when he came on as a substitute in the last Premier League game of the 2001/02 season?

1   Which one of the following was not a
    founder member of the football league:
    Liverpool, Aston Villa, West Bromwich
    Albion?

2   Neil Redfearn holds the record number
    of Premier League appearances for which
    club?

3   Which former Premier League team's
    ground features the Pukka Pies Stand and
    the Lookers Stand?

4   Who in December 2001, scored the
    Premier League's 10,000th goal?

5   Can you name either of the two
    Tottenham Hotspur players since 2002
    whose surnames start with the letter Z?

6   Which former Everton player is, up to the
    start of 2004, the only Premier League
    player whose surname starts with the
    letter 'X'?

7   And which country has the above
    footballer played for?

MEDIUM ———— REGULAR SEASON

8 How many times did Robbie Fowler score a hat-trick in a Premier League match for Liverpool?

9 Which former England captain holds the record as the oldest player to represent Middlesbrough in the Premier League?

10 Against which side did Chelsea's lowest Premier League attendance (8923) occur?

11 Against which current Premier League side has Southampton never lost at home in all ten matches?

12 What was the name of the 1994 report that advised the closing of standing terracing in Premier League grounds?

13 Which season saw the arrival of three substitutes without restriction: 1992/93, 1995/96, 1997/98 or 1998/99?

14 If you were sitting in the Gwladys Stand, would you be at Everton, Aston Villa or Portsmouth?

15 For which country does Mustapha Hadji play international football?

116

16 Ashley Ward has played for five different Premier League clubs. Can you name two of them?

17 Who started his career with Tottenham Hotspur, before playing for both Liverpool and Everton in the Premier League?

18 Which well-known Premier League striker was signed by Aston Villa from Signal Hill in 1989?

19 Who was named both the Players' and the Football Writers' Footballer of the Year in April 2001?

20 Which Premier League team was knocked out of the third round of the 2003/04 FA Cup by Gillingham?

21 For which club was Tony Cottee playing when they won the Worthington Cup and secured his first ever winner's medal after seventeen years of trying?

22 In their eight seasons in the Premier League, how many times did Wimbledon's leading goal scorer not reach ten or more goals?

23 If you were sitting in the Revie Stand, would you be at Leeds United, Birmingham City or West Bromwich Albion?

24 Did Oldham Athletic's four Premier League games against Chelsea, Liverpool or Manchester United see them collect three wins and one draw?

25 Which one of the following was not a founder member of the football league: Wolverhampton Wanderers, Derby County, Arsenal?

26 Against which fellow north-east England side have Middlesbrough won just two Premier League matches in fifteen attempts?

27 What is given if a goalkeeper holds onto the ball in his penalty area for more than six seconds?

28 Which Premier League team's nickname stems from a sweet factory nearby?

29 Who played almost 300 League games for Charlton before joining Newcastle United?

30 Former Arsenal and Sunderland defender Steve Bould now owns a chain of garden furniture stores: true or false?

31 Norwegian Egil Olsen was manager of which team in the season they were last relegated from the Premier League?

32 In 1999/2000, which famous striker was sent off in the Premier League for the first time?

33 Which team has scored more Premier League goals against Middlesbrough than any other side?

34 Which former Manchester United, Chelsea and Southampton footballer was nicknamed 'Sparky'?

35 Which team has never beaten Chelsea in their 23 Premier League encounters up to the start of 2004?

36 For which former Premier League team does Mark Bright hold the record number of goals?

37 Which team had 22 different players booked and six sent off in both the 2000/01 and 2001/02 seasons?

38 From which country does Blackburn Rovers forward Brett Emerton come?

39 Which club's transfer record was broken in 2000 with the signing of Dutch striker, Nordin Wooter for £950,000?

40 Which former Premier League team's fans are nicknamed 'the Tractor Boys'?

41 Which Premier League team signed eighteen-year-old Chinese striker, Dong Fangzhou in January 2004?

42 Whose record Premier League defeat was an 8-0 thrashing by Newcastle United in 1999?

43 Which 2003/04 side were first called Small Heath Alliance when they formed in 1875?

44 In the 1996/97 season which Premier League side did York City knock out of the FA Cup?

45 Which winger in the Premier League is named after a former US President?

46 Against which side did Arsenal draw its lowest ever Premier League home attendance of 18,253?

47 Which central defender played in every Premier League game of the 1992/93 and 1994/95 seasons for Manchester United?

48 Former Everton player Trevor Steven now owns a children's shoe shop in Glasgow: true or false?

49 Which team dramatically beat Liverpool in the last game of the 1999/2000 season to stay in the Premier League?

50 Which TV pundit has a stand named after him at the Walkers Stadium?

🖤🖤 **REGULAR SEASON QUIZ 18** 🖤🖤

1 Which Manchester United star played for England Schoolboys before becoming a full international with Wales?

2 Up to the start of 2004, was Sylvain Wiltord, Thierry Henry or Robert Pires the most expensive signing Arsenal have ever made?

3 Which Leeds United player scored four goals against Liverpool in their 4-3 win in 2000?

4 For which club has Alan Shearer notched up nine Premier League hat-tricks?

5 Which current Premier League club's lowest ever attendance saw just over 9000 people watch a 1993/94 game against Ipswich Town?

6 What relationship is Harry Redknapp to Jamie Redknapp: father, uncle or cousin?

7 Up to the start of 2004, Chelsea have been beaten by four or more goals in the Premier League once, twice, three or four times?

8 Which player, since then a Premier League manager, holds the record for the oldest player on the pitch for Leeds United?

9 In which season did Aston Villa have 24 different players booked during Premier League games?

10 Former Leeds United striker Lee Chapman is studying to be a psychologist: true or false?

11 Which long-serving Everton defender had one season at West Ham in 1997/98 before returning to Goodison Park?

12 In 1997/98, it became possible to score a goal directly from what situation?

13 Which club's record signing when in the Premier League cost £1.5 million from Partizan Belgrade?

14 Which Chelsea player has over 110 caps for France?

15 Which team's ground features an Itchen Stand and a Chapel Stand?

16 Which holder of the Turkish record for international goals scored, joined Blackburn in the 2002/03 season?

17 Which player cost Manchester United the most: Roy Keane, Eric Djemba-Djemba, Peter Schmeichel, Henning Berg?

18 Who holds the record for the most Premier League appearances at Arsenal?

19 How many different Middlesbrough players scored penalties in the Premier League in the 1999/2000 season?

20 In 2001/02 Chelsea won how many Premier League games by a four-goal margin?

21 Stuart McCall holds the record of 71 Premier League appearances for which club?

22 From which country does Manchester United's Eric Djemba-Djemba come?

23 Which club bought Ade Akinbayi for £3 million and sold him less than a year later for £5 million?

24 Which defender has made the most Premier League appearances for Leeds United?

25 Which current Premier League club's first ever game in 1874 was played with one half under football rules and the other half using rugby rules?

26 Which famous Premier League club's first ever victory came over 100 years ago when they were called Dial Square and beat Eastern Wanderers 6-0?

27 Which former Premier League club was founded as Singers in 1883: Oldham Athletic, Coventry City or Sheffield United?

28 For which team was Gary Croft playing when he became the first English footballer to wear an electronic tag whilst playing a professional match?

29 Arsenal have only had one Premier League loss by five or more goals. In which season was it?

30 Did the backpass law, not allowing keepers to handle the ball, come into effect in the Premier League's first, second, third or fifth season?

31 Which former Premier League team's ground lies next to the River Trent?

32 What country does El Hadji Diouf come from: Morocco, Senegal, Algeria or Nigeria?

33 How many seasons did Jamie Redknapp play for Liverpool in the Premier League?

34 Which Premier League club let three goalkeepers leave the club in the summer of 2003?

35 Can you name two of the three goalkeepers?

36 The 1993/1994 season saw Liverpool's lowest ever Premier League attendance but against which side?

37 Which club in the 1998/99 season had nineteen different Premier League goal scorers but with no player reaching ten goals?

38 Italian striker, Atillo Lombardo was briefly manager of which team in the Premier League?

39 Belgian football club Royal Antwerp acts as a feeder club for which Premier League team?

40 Whose record win in the Premier League came in 1995 when they beat Leeds United 6-2?

41 Former Manchester United player Norman Whiteside is now a podiatrist: true or false?

42 Which two teams played in the match that holds the record for the lowest ever attendance at a Premier League game?

43 Was the attendance for that match: 3039, 5119, 7469 or 8309?

44 What is the name of the Premier League ground with two sides of its ground called the Riverside Stand and the Darwen End?

45 In the 1995/96 season which team had four players who scored ten or more Premier League goals?

46 Which team paid £5 million for a Spanish defender with the first name Elena?

47 Middlesbrough's Massimo Maccarone comes from which country?

48 Against which team has Tottenham Hotspur never drawn and only lost twice in their ten matches?

49 As of the start of 2004, which team has scored more Premier League goals against Manchester United than any other side?

50 For which team was goalkeeper John Burridge playing when he became their eldest ever Premier League player at the age of 43 years and five months?

◉◉ REGULAR SEASON QUIZ 19 ◉◉

1 Which former Premier League team played its 2003/04 games at the National Hockey Stadium?

2 Which Liverpool player was fined £900 in March 1997 for displaying a t-shirt with a political protest message underneath his match shirt?

3 From what country did Graeme Souness return to England in order to manage Southampton?

4 What was the surname of the three brothers, Rodney, Ray and Danny who all played football at Southampton?

5 Much-travelled striker, Steve Claridge was which Premier League club's top goal scorer in 1996/97?

6 Which Manchester United star announced a shock early retirement in May 1997?

7 In the last game of the 1996/97 season, which relegated team did Newcastle beat 5-0 to finish in second place?

8 Which team only managed to keep three clean sheets during the 1994/95 season?

9 Which team has lost only twice to Aston Villa and beaten them eleven times in 21 Premier League encounters?

10 What is Arsenal manager Arsène Wenger's nickname in the dressing room?

11 What is the name of famous Premier League goalkeeper's son on the books at Manchester City?

12 And what position does he play?

13 Against which current Premier League side has Liverpool never won in eleven matches away from home?

14 QPR players have scored four Premier League hat-tricks, three of which were against the same team. Can you name it?

15 Wendy Toms, Karen Brady or Lindsay Cartwright was the first female referee's assistant in the Premier League?

16 Which 2003/04 Premier League side has to travel more miles (7934) than any other in order to play its nineteen away matches?

17 Who was the last English manager to win the Premier League?

18 What is the name given to the Spanish equivalent of the Premier League?

19 Leicester City have never won a Premier League home game against which side, in eight attempts?

20 Former Arsenal goalkeeper, TV pundit and Arsenal goalkeeping coach Bob Wilson's middle name is Ferguson, Primrose or Wembley?

21 Sean Davis played for which club in all three English divisions and the Premier League?

22 Which Southampton defender played 284 games for the club before scoring his first goal: Francis Benali, Wayne Bridge or Jason Dodd?

23 Which Manchester United youngster made his debut for England after playing just eleven first team games for his club side?

24 Which Premier League striker released an R'n'B single called Outstanding, in 2000?

25 Who managed his own son whilst Coventry City were in the Premier League?

26 Which England goalkeeper retired from football in January 2004?

27 Which former Manchester United and Chelsea midfielder was the oldest player to represent QPR in the Premier League?

28 Birmingham-based company, Hudson & Co. are the leading manufacturer of referee's whistles, goalposts or footballs used in the Premier League?

29 President of UEFA, Lennart Johansson, supports which Premier League team: Arsenal, Liverpool or Southampton?

30 Against which side did David Seaman play his last Premier League match before retiring?

31 An injury to what part of his body in the above match saw David Seaman leave the field after thirteen minutes?

32 Swindon Town managed to score a goal against all but one of the teams in their only Premier League season. Can you name the team?

33 Which club, recently relegated from the Premier League, was once known by the name Thames Ironworks FC?

34 Who was Arsenal's second leading goal scorer in the 2002/03 season: Thierry Henry, Robert Pires, Sylvain Wiltord or Kanu?

35 Which Premier League side did second division Tranmere Rovers knock out of the 2004 FA Cup third round?

36 In their two seasons in the Premier League, Oldham Athletic lost all four games to only one club. Was it Blackburn Rovers, Liverpool or Arsenal?

37 As of the start of 2004, which side has scored more goals against Arsenal than any other?

38 Which Premier League player was top scorer in the Champions League in the 2002/03 season?

39 Which goalkeeper holds the record for the most appearances in the Premier League as of the start of the 2003/04 season?

40 Tottenham's Les Ferdinand scored the Premier League's 10,000th goal in a 4-0 victory over Fulham, Barnsley, Southampton or Charlton Athletic?

41 Who scored the Premier League's first ever hat-trick when his side beat Tottenham 5-0 in August 1992?

42 And who was he playing for at the time?

43 Who currently holds the Chelsea record for the most Premier League goals scored?

44 Was Efan Ekoku, Ian Wright, Ian Rush or Jason Euell the first player to score four goals in a single Premier League game?

45 Who scored a hat-trick on the opening day of the 1995/96 season but ended up on the losing side when Southampton lost 4-3 to Nottingham Forest?

46 Ten seconds into a game, defender, Ledley King scored his first ever goal and one of the Premier League's fastest – but for which club?

47 Which one of the following was not a founder member of the football league: Blackburn Rovers, Stoke City or Chelsea?

48 Were Bolton Wanderers, Crystal Palace or Manchester City the first club to be relegated from the Premier League twice?

49 Which French defender has played in Serie A for Inter Milan, in the Spanish League for Barcelona and in the Premier League for Manchester United?

50 Which player moved from Charlton to Chelsea in January 2004 for approximately £12 million?

TOUGH TO TACKLE

1. How many Premier League points did Sunderland obtain during the part of the 2002/03 season when they were managed by Howard Wilkinson?

2. Can you name the other two managers who managed Sunderland during the 2002/03 season?

3. Who was the unlucky fourth team to be relegated in the one year where the Premier League numbers were reduced from 22 to 20?

4. Of all the teams that have played in the Premier League, which was the last to join the professional English leagues?

5. How many teams relegated in the 1993/94 season have since returned to the Premier League?

6 Can you name the Premier League manager who entered the 2003 UK Open Darts championship?

7 During the 1998/99 season, which two Premier League teams played each other six times, five of the games occurring in just six weeks?

8 How many seasons did David Seaman have at Arsenal, joining after four seasons at QPR, two at Birmingham City and three at Peterborough United?

9 In 2002/03, which team scored more goals from outside the penalty area than any other team?

10 Which former Premier League team's name is the only one in the English league starting with five consonants?

11 How many of teams relegated in the 1992/93 season have since returned to the Premier League?

12 Can you name either of the 1995/96 teams which finished on 38 points, the same as a relegated side?

13 Which team drew more games than any other team in the 1996/97 season?

14 In 1997/98, which team finished level on points with Bolton but were not relegated because they had a superior goal difference?

15 Only one former Premier League club's name does not contain any of the letters you would find in the word 'mackerel'. Can you name it?

16 Which Premier League player came on as a substitute and replaced his own father, Arnor, in an international match between Iceland and Estonia?

17 Up to the end of the 2003 season, Norwich's Ruel Fox – in 1993 – was the last person to do what at Old Trafford in the Premier League?

18 Which goalkeeper, now at QPR, has the shortest Manchester United first team career of any player, having played just 75 seconds against Arsenal at Highbury in August 1999?

19 Which two teams in 2003 featured Chinese footballers causing over 300 million people in China to watch their New Year's Day game?

20 Swindon collected all six points against only one Premier League rival. Which team was it?

21 Which Premier League player won the FIFA Fair Play Award in 2000 for his work with children and fighting racism?

22 Which member of Charlton's 2003/04 squad has already received more than 50 international caps for Bulgaria?

23 Which long-serving Arsenal defender, recently retired, is a rare example of an English Premier League player with an 'X' in his name?

24 Who was awarded Manager of the Year in 2001, the first time that the award had been won by a manager whose team did not win the Premier League?

25 In what season did all three relegated teams share the same second name?

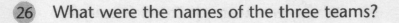

26 What were the names of the three teams?

27 Of the thirteen players brought into Chelsea between June and August 2003, which was the most expensive?

28 What was the average age of a Premier League footballer during the 2002/03 season?

29 Which Sheffield United player scored the very first Premier League goal?

30 Which Premier League club was called Ardwick in the distant past?

31 Against which team did Jan-Aage Fjortoft hit Swindon Town's only Premier League hat-trick?

32 Five current and former Premier League sides do not share their second names with another club in the Premier League or three Nationwide divisions. Can you name three of them?

33 Which Charlton Athletic player was phoned up by Nelson Mandela, who wanted an invitation to his wedding?

34 What percentage of Premier League games of the 2002/03 season were goalless: 6%, 11% 18% or 24%?

35 Only one former Premier League club does not share the third word of its name with any other team in the Premier and three Nationwide leagues. Can you name it?

36 Which goalkeeper injured himself in the 1999/2000 season when he dropped a bottle of salad cream on his foot?

37 What nationality is Blackburn Rovers defender, Vratislav Gresko?

38 Which Premier League manager sold his own son for £250,000 to Wolverhampton Wanderers?

39 At the start of 2004, only one player has ever scored in a Manchester Derby, a Merseyside Derby and a Glasgow Derby. Who is he?

40 Two of the three 2002/03 players whose surnames started with the letter 'Q' played in the North East. Can you name both of them?

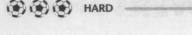

41 Which former Manchester United player is the Czech Republic's most-capped player?

42 What was the name of Manchester United's first ever American goalkeeper?

43 Who brought Chris Sutton to Chelsea for £10 million then sold him for £6 million?

44 Which goalkeeper played for nineteen different English league clubs?

45 From which country does Southampton's Agustin Delgardo hail?

46 How much did West Ham pay for Ian Wright when Arsenal sold him?

47 Which former Tottenham Hotspur player was the Ukraine's most capped player?

48 Which former Premier League club was once called St Judes?

49 Who scored 99 goals for Arsenal?

50 Who is the tallest ever Premier League striker?

ANSWERS

1. 20
2. Three
3. Manchester United
4. Everton
5. Arsenal
6. Chelsea
7. Sir Alex Ferguson
8. Liverpool
9. 1992
10. Gordon Strachan
11. A volley
12. David Beckham
13. Real Madrid
14. Wolverhampton, Bolton
15. False
16. Louis Saha
17. Tottenham Hotspur
18. Liverpool and Everton
19. Arsène Wenger
20. Portsmouth
21. 22
22. Gary and Phil Neville
23. Sheffield Wednesday
24. Southampton
25. Michael Owen
26. Three
27. None
28. Roy Keane
29. Liverpool
30. Three
31. Manchester United
32. True
33. France
34. Wimbledon
35. Arsenal and Tottenham Hotspur
36. Manchester United
37. Greece
38. Goalkeeper's throws
39. Arsenal
40. Chelsea
41. Drop-ball
42. Alan Shearer
43. Eric Cantona
44. The Netherlands
45. Wimbledon
46. White
47. All of the ball
48. Manchester United
49. Portsmouth
50. David Beckham

Regular Season Quiz 1
1. Blackburn Rovers
2. West Bromwich Albion
3. Graham le Saux
4. Alan Curbishley
5. Aston Villa
6. Alan Shearer and Les Ferdinand
7. Coventry City
8. Arsenal
9. Wimbledon
10. 1997/98
11. Harry Kewell
12. Charlton
13. Andy Cole
14. Robbie Keane
15. Bryan Robson
16. Ipswich Town
17. Crystal Palace

18. Kevin Phillips
19. Tony Yeboah
20. Fulham
21. Blackburn Rovers
22. They have all been Premier League referees
23. 7-0
24. Bolton Wanderers
25. 1941
26. Welsh
27. Robbie Keane
28. Blue and white
29. Emile Heskey
30. West Bromwich Albion
31. Manchester City
32. Arsène Wenger
33. Preston North End
34. False
35. Sunderland
36. Sunderland
37. Blackburn Rovers
38. 2002/03
39. Sunderland
40. Leicester City
41. Manchester United
42. Blackburn Rovers
43. Niall Quinn
44. 14th
45. Manchester United
46. Arsenal, Fulham and Southampton
47. Liverpool
48. Sheffield United
49. Ian Wright
50. They were all headers

Regular Season Quiz 2
1. True
2. The Play Offs
3. Tim Howerd
4. Bradford City
5. Own goals
6. True

7. 2002
8. Manchester United
9. Leicester City
10. False
11. Arsenal
12. Sunderland
13. Fulham
14. True
15. Nigeria
16. West Ham
17. European Cup-Winners Cup
18. Birmingham City
19. Southampton
20. Three
21. Everton, Arsenal, Nottingham Forest
22. Wolverhampton Wanderers
23. Never
24. Ruud Gullit
25. Fulham
26. Manchester United
27. Terry Venables
28. Coventry City
29. West Ham United
30. Two
31. Two
32. European Cup-Winners Cup
33. South Africa
34. Portsmouth
35. James Milner and Wayne Rooney
36. Oldham Athletic
37. Queens Park Rangers
38. West Ham
39. Two (The Valley – Charlton Athletic, Valley Parade – Bradford City)
40. Liverpool
41. One
42. George Graham
43. Triangular
44. Manchester United
45. Chelsea

46. Sir Alex Ferguson
47. Fulham
48. Barnsley
49. Manchester City
50. Five

Regular Season Quiz 3
1. Two
2. Manchester United, Tottenham Hotspur and Portsmouth
3. Aston Villa
4. Paolo Di Canio
5. Sheffield United
6. Ledley King
7. Everton
8. Uruguay
9. Wimbledon
10. Marc-Vivien Foe
11. Benito Carbone
12. Columbus Crew
13. Norwich City
14. Tony Yeboah
15. Wolverhampton Wanderers
16. Everton
17. Sporting Chance
18. Sheffield Wednesday
19. The Fourth Official
20. Chris Coleman
21. 1999
22. Ruud Gullit
23. Manchester United
24. Stuart Pearce
25. The Canaries
26. Thierry Henry
27. Rio Ferdinand
28. Manchester City
29. Alex Ferguson
30. Manchester City
31. Ten
32. Eric Cantona
33. Four
34. Nottingham Forest
35. Signing

36. Bolton Wanderers
37. Michael Owen
38. Crystal Palace
39. Jamie Carragher
40. Wolverhampton Wanderers
41. Dion Dublin
42. David Beckham
43. Robert Pires
44. Kenny Dalglish
45. Six
46. Manchester City
47. Kasey Keller
48. Villa Park
49. Leeds United
50. Liverpool

Regular Season Quiz 4
1. Norwich City
2. Alan Shearer
3. Arsenal
4. Gary Megson
5. Craig Bellamy
6. Eight
7. Ian Wright
8. Portsmouth
9. 38
10. Nottingham Forest
11. Marcus Stewart
12. Charlton Athletic
13. Aston Villa
14. Barnsley
15. Graeme Souness
16. Fulham
17. Jermaine Jenas
18. Everton
19. Paul Gascoigne
20. Aston Villa
21. Ipswich Town and Norwich City
22. Crystal Palace
23. Celtic
24. Manchester United, Manchester City and Aston Villa

25. Tore Andre Flo
26. One
27. Aston Villa
28. Fabrizio Ravanelli
29. Manchester City
30. Damien Duff
31. Tottenham Hotspur
32. Gareth Southgate
33. Sheffield Wednesday, Aston Villa, Bradford City, Derby County, Middlesbrough
34. Everton
35. Manchester United
36. None
37. Chelsea
38. Jim Smith
39. Queens Park Rangers
40. Olof Mellberg
41. Chelsea
42. Arsenal
43. Ruud van Nistelrooy
44. Howard Kendall
45. Four times
46. Wimbledon
47. Sunderland
48. Sam Allardyce
49. Wayne Rooney
50. Wimbledon

Regular Season Quiz 5
1. Sunderland
2. Gianfranco Zola
3. West Ham
4. West Bromwich Albion
5. Lee Bowyer
6. Thierry Henry
7. Arsenal
8. Aston Villa
9. Blackburn Rovers
10. £30 million
11. Middlesbrough
12. Everton
13. Queens Park Rangers
14. Norwich City
15. Juan Sebastian Veron
16. Watford
17. Robbie Fowler
18. Leeds United, Liverpool, Aston Villa
19. Arsenal
20. Manchester United
21. A goalkeeper
22. Charlton Athletic
23. Alan Smith
24. Ruud Gullit
25. Middlesbrough
26. Queens Park Rangers
27. Thirteen
28. Everton
29. Nicholas Anelka
30. Portman Road
31. Aston Villa
32. Sheffield United
33. Eddie Gray
34. True
35. Ian Wright
36. David Seaman
37. True
38. Teddy Sheringham
39. Arsenal
40. Roker Park
41. Matt Le Tissier
42. Thierry Henry
43. Arsenal
44. Clive Allen
45. Aston Villa
46. No team
47. Liverpool
48. 18
49. Vinnie Jones
50. Argentina

Regular Season Quiz 6
1. Manchester United
2. Wycombe Wanderers
3. Peter Schmeichel

4. Liverpool
5. Robert Pires, for Arsenal
6. Everton
7. Fulham
8. Micky Adams
9. Paulo Wanchope
10. David Beckham
11. West Ham United
12. Aston Villa
13. 1997/98
14. Wolverhampton Wanderers and Southampton
15. Newcastle United
16. Fred The Red
17. Ipswich Town
18. Chelsea and Arsenal
19. Charlton Athletic
20. West Ham United
21. Ayresome Park
22. David Pleat
23. Chelsea
24. Liverpool
25. Joe Kinnear
26. Mark Crossley
27. Liverpool
28. One month
29. Manchester United
30. Denis Irwin, Paul Ince
31. Niall Quinn
32. Dwight Yorke
33. Alan Shearer
34. Charlton Athletic
35. Ipswich Town
36. Liverpool
37. West Ham United
38. Two
39. Wayne Rooney
40. Sheffield United, Southampton, Manchester City
41. Old Trafford
42. Burnden Park
43. Four
44. Three
45. One point
46. George Weah
47. Manchester City and Chelsea
48. Blackburn Rovers (6-1)
49. Sheffield Wednesday
50. Kevin Phillips

Regular Season Quiz 7
1. Liverpool
2. David O'Leary
3. Southampton
4. Rio Ferdinand
5. Brian Kidd
6. 7-1
7. Queens Park Rangers
8. 1994/95
9. David Unsworth
10. Liverpool Football Club
11. Nicolas Anelka
12. Kieron Dyer, Richard Wright
13. Graham Taylor
14. Les Ferdinand
15. Third place (2001/02 season)
16. Thierry Henry
17. Birmingham City
18. Alan Shearer
19. Ipswich Town
20. John Hartson
21. True
22. Linesmen
23. Martin O'Neill
24. Peruvian
25. Alan Stubbs
26. Fulham
27. Newcastle United
28. £13 million
29. David O'Leary, Eddie Gray, Terry Venables and Peter Reid
30. The Charity Shield
31. Six
32. Liverpool
33. Swindon

34. Three – Manchester
    City/United, West
    Ham/Bromwich Albion and
    Sheffield Wednesday/United
35. Arsenal
36. Swindon
37. Never
38. Mark Viduka
39. Two
40. Eric Cantona
41. Monaco
42. Bolton Wanderers
43. Southampton
44. Leicester City
45. Nicolas Anelka
46. Senegal
47. Blackburn Rovers
48. Leeds United
49. Liverpool
50. West Ham United

Regular Season Quiz 8
1. Frank Lampard
2. False
3. Scottish
4. Norwich City
5. Gianfranco Zola
6. 1999
7. 1994
8. Everton
9. Willie Carson
10. Stephen Clemence, son of Ray
11. Ruud van Nistelrooy
12. Gilberto Silva
13. Queens Park Rangers
14. Steven Gerrard
15. Stan Collymore
16. Brad Friedel
17. Chris Sutton
18. Shaun Goater
19. Aston Villa
20. Bryan Robson
21. Tottenham Hotspur

22. Highbury
23. James Beattie
24. Newcastle United
25. Middlesbrough
26. Leicester City
27. Peter Crouch
28. Everton
29. 0
30. Two
31. Nottingham Forest
32. Birmingham
33. Sven Goran Eriksson
34. 1995/96
35. Over 60
36. Jenny Agutter
37. Arsenal
38. Robbie Fowler
39. Liverpool
40. 92
41. Ian Wright
42. St James Park (Newcastle United)
43. Ole Gunnar Solskjaer
44. Nottingham Forest
45. Three
46. West Ham United
47. One
48. None
49. Walter Smith
50. Arsenal

Regular Season Quiz 9
1. Sheffield United
2. Derby County
3. Leeds United
4. Twice
5. Nottingham Forest
6. Alan Shearer
7. 10
8. Paul Konchesky
9. Fulham
10. Roy Evans
11. Swindon Town

12. Southampton, Chelsea and Manchester United, Everton, Blackburn Rovers
13. Ruud van Nistelrooy
14. Leicester City
15. Tottenham Hotspur
16. Number of red cards
17. Norwich City
18. James Beattie
19. Four
20. Robert Pires
21. Argentina
22. Coventry City
23. Manchester United
24. Alan Shearer
25. Leeds United
26. The Dell
27. Everton
28. Sunderland
29. Chelsea
30. Manchester City
31. 2003
32. Paul Ince
33. Franco Baresi
34. Jimmy Floyd Hasselbaink
35. Birmingham City
36. Sunderland
37. Junichi Inamoto
38. Bruce Rioch
39. Harry Kewell
40. Sheffield Wednesday and Barnsley
41. Charlton Athletic
42. Leeds United
43. Blackburn Rovers
44. Joe Royle
45. Twelve
46. Manchester
47. Derby County
48. Leeds United
49. Manchester United
50. Sweden

Regular Season Quiz 10
1. Manchester United
2. Michael Owen
3. Thierry Henry
4. Mark Hughes
5. West Ham
6. Terry Venables
7. Six
8. Ole Gunnar Solskaer
9. Arsenal
10. Francis Jeffers
11. John Motson
12. Crystal Palace and Nottingham Forest
13. Manchester United
14. Harry Kewell
15. Sunderland
16. Chelsea
17. Sunderland
18. Oldham Athletic
19. Danny Mills and Lee Bowyer
20. Derby County
21. Southampton
22. True
23. David James
24. Paul Scholes
25. 2001
26. David Moyes
27. Ryan Giggs
28. Once
29. Liverpool, Blackburn Rovers, Bolton Wanderers
30. Sheffield Wednesday
31. Liverpool
32. West Ham United
33. Sol Campbell
34. Arsenal
35. Marconi Stallions
36. Liverpool
37. Ryan Giggs
38. Jimmy Floyd Hasselbaink, Ruud van Nistelrooy, Alan Shearer

39. Roy Keane
40. Wayne Bridge
41. Leicester City, Norwich City
42. Brian Clough
43. Leicester City
44. 35,500
45. Third
46. Middlesbrough
47. Third place (1999/2000 season)
48. Peter Ridsdale
49. Scotland
50. Tottenham Hotspur

Regular Season Quiz 11
1. Manchester United, Newcastle United
2. Alan Curbishley
3. 2000/01
4. Play a penalty shootout
5. Bradford City
6. Tottenham Hotspur
7. Nottingham Forest
8. Six
9. Sunderland
10. Colin Cameron
11. Matt Le Tissier
12. Fulham
13. 2001
14. Peter Schmeichel, David Seaman
15. Chelsea
16. Brian Kidd and Steve McLaren
17. Emmanuel Petit
18. Ole Gunnar Solskjaer
19. Sheffield Wednesday and Bradford City
20. Tottenham Hotspur
21. Nolberto Solano
22. Watford
23. Paulo di Canio
24. Leeds United
25. Sunderland
26. Fulham

27. Steve Bruce
28. Portsmouth
29. Manchester United
30. It was the first time the team included no English players
31. Patrick Viera
32. The Reebok
33. He was a defender
34. Sir Jack Hayward
35. Swindon Town
36. Alan Hansen
37. Glenn Hoddle
38. Steve McClaren
39. Wimbledon
40. West Ham United
41. Southampton
42. Three
43. Everton
44. Nicky Butt
45. Lee Bowyer
46. Peter Reid
47. Dwight Yorke
48. Gary Lineker
49. Wimbledon
50. Neil Sullivan

Regular Season Quiz 12
1. Swindon Town
2. The Commonwealth Games (2002)
3. Wolverhampton Wanderers
4. Norwich City
5. Bayern Munich
6. Robbie Fowler
7. Dennis Bergkamp (after Denis Law)
8. Nick Barmby
9. Nicolas Anelka, playing for Liverpool and then Manchester City
10. Manchester United
11. Barnsley
12. Wolverhampton Wanderers

13. Chelsea
14. Sunderland
15. Leeds United
16. 1999/2000
17. Faustino Asprilla
18. Eight
19. Oldham Athletic
20. Jordi Cruyff
21. Queens Park Rangers
22. Israeli
23. Derby County
24. Two
25. Birmingham City
26. Six goals
27. Blackburn Rovers, Newcastle United
28. Newcastle United
29. Manchester City
30. Newcastle United
31. Leeds United
32. Southampton
33. Ron Atkinson
34. Manchester United
35. Mark Hughes
36. Francis Jeffers
37. Five
38. Mikael Silvestre
39. Chelsea
40. Newcastle United
41. Tottenham Hotspur
42. George Graham, Bruce Rioch
43. True
44. Newcastle United
45. Alan Shearer
46. John Hartson
47. Paul Ince
48. Kenny Dalglish
49. True
50. Everton's ground, Goodison Park

Regular Season Quiz 13
1. One
2. Eidur Gudjohnsen
3. Middlesbrough
4. Watford
5. Alan Smith
6. Fulham
7. Norwich, Everton
8. Leeds United
9. Frank Lampard
10. Newcastle United
11. Gary Speed
12. Dennis Bergkamp
13. Three - Aston Villa, Charlton Athletic and Liverpool
14. Jimmy Floyd Hasselbaink
15. Michael Owen, Dwight Yorke
16. Eric Cantona
17. Swindon Town
18. Newcastle United
19. Arsenal
20. Newcastle United
21. Millennium Stadium, Cardiff
22. 1998/99 season
23. Howard Wilkinson
24. Arsenal
25. Republic of Ireland
26. Luke Chadwick
27. Oldham Athletic
28. Carlos Queiroz
29. Matt Le Tissier
30. Wolverhampton Wanderers
31. Nine
32. True (Lee Holmes, 15 years 268 days)
33. Ryan Giggs
34. West Bromwich Albion
35. Two
36. George Graham, David O'Leary, Terry Venables, Peter Reid
37. Aston Villa, Leicester City

38. Nottingham Forest
39. Ruud van Nistelrooy
40. Danny Murphy
41. Trevor Brooking
42. Manchester United
43. Michael Owen
44. Eight
45. Shay Given
46. Blackburn Rovers
47. Charlton Athletic and West Ham United
48. Sheffield Wednesday
49. Uriah Rennie
50. Tottenham Hotspur

Regular Season Quiz 14
1. Stan Collymore
2. Arsenal
3. Ole Gunnar Solskjaer
4. Ruud van Nistelrooy
5. Wimbledon
6. Barnsley
7. Tottenham Hotspur, Queens Park Rangers
8. Chelsea
9. Manchester City
10. Kevin Phillips
11. Alan Shearer
12. Michael Owen
13. January
14. Middlesbrough
15. 11m
16. Terry Venables
17. Luis Boa Morte
18. Aston Villa
19. Denis Irwin
20. Kanu
21. Switzerland
22. Nottingham Forest
23. Barnsley
24. Paul Merson
25. Leeds United
26. Les Ferdinand

27. Bolton Wanderers, Middlesbrough
28. John Aldridge
29. Sheffield Wednesday
30. Kevin Pressman
31. Leicester City
32. Czech Republic
33. Play advantage
34. Blackburn Rovers
35. Chelsea
36. Serie A
37. Dion Dublin
38. Canada
39. 9m
40. Sir Bobby Robson
41. His 71st
42. Southampton
43. Paul Scholes
44. Ian Porterfield
45. Charlton Athletic
46. Bolton Wanderers
47. Seven
48. Teddy Sheringham
49. Newcastle United
50. Trevor Francis

Regular Season Quiz 15
1. Southampton
2. Osvaldo Ardiles, Christian Gross
3. A goal kick
4. Jens Lehmann
5. Ruud van Nistelrooy
6. Canada
7. John Gregory
8. 2001
9. Charlton Athletic
10. Charlton Athletic
11. Kolo Toure
12. Colombia
13. Tottenham Hotspur
14. Leeds United
15. Shaka Hislop

16. Tottenham Hotspur
17. Kasey Keller
18. Bundesliga
19. Robbie Keane
20. Wolverhampton Wanderers
21. Arsenal
22. Mart Poom
23. Andy Cole
24. Chelsea
25. None
26. Three
27. Norwich City, Manchester City, Coventry City
28. First
29. Watford
30. Crystal Palace
31. Derby County
32. Queens Park Rangers
33. An indirect free kick
34. No
35. A free transfer
36. The third round
37. Aston Villa
38. Mick Harford
39. Gary Neville
40. Four
41. Alan Shearer
42. Managing director
43. Mark Hughes
44. Leeds United
45. Nutmeg
46. False
47. Brighton and Hove Albion
48. Danny Mills
49. Manchester United
50. Chelsea

Regular Season Quiz 16
1. Chelsea
2. Wales
3. Marian Pahars
4. Arsenal
5. Paulo Wanchope

6. Karl Power
7. Aston Villa
8. Both
9. Leeds United
10. Edu
11. Michael Tarnat
12. 2000/01
13. Five
14. St Andrews (Birmingham City)
15. Blackburn Rovers
16. Stuart Gray
17. Southampton
18. Manchester United, Wimbledon
19. Fulham
20. Arsenal
21. South Africa
22. One
23. Dwight Yorke
24. Manchester City
25. Mark Bright
26. To be played indoors
27. Southampton
28. Liverpool
29. Norwich City
30. Arsenal
31. Sheffield Wednesday
32. Bolton Wanderers
33. Michael Owen
34. Manchester United
35. Robbie Fowler
36. Six
37. Les Ferdinand
38. Dennis Bergkamp
39. Six
40. Four
41. Robert Lee, Les Ferdinand, Alan Shearer
42. Five
43. Gordon Strachan
44. Eyal Berkovic
45. Jermaine Jenas
46. Cristiano Ronaldo

47. Fulham, Arsenal, Southampton
48. Aston Villa
49. Liverpool, Villa, Leicester, Notts Forest, Bradford
50. Raimond van der Gouw

Regular Season Quiz 17
1. Liverpool
2. Barnsley
3. Oldham Athletic
4. Les Ferdinand
5. Bobby Zamora, Christian Ziege
6. Abel Xavier
7. Portugal
8. Eight times
9. Bryan Robson
10. Coventry City
11. Newcastle United
12. The Taylor Report
13. 1995/96
14. Everton
15. Morocco
16. Norwich, Derby County, Barnsley, Blackburn Rovers, Bradford City
17. Nick Barmby
18. Dwight Yorke
19. Teddy Sheringham
20. Charlton Athletic
21. Leicester City
22. Three times
23. Leeds United
24. Chelsea
25. Arsenal
26. Newcastle United
27. An indirect free kick
28. Everton (The Toffees)
29. Robert Lee
30. False
31. Wimbledon
32. Alan Shearer
33. Arsenal
34. Mark Hughes

35. Tottenham Hotspur
36. Sheffield Wednesday
37. Middlesbrough
38. Australia
39. Watford
40. Ipswich Town
41. Manchester United
42. Sheffield Wednesday
43. Birmingham City
44. Everton
45. Cristiano Ronaldo (after Ronald Reagan)
46. Wimbledon
47. Gary Pallister
48. True
49. Bradford City
50. Gary Lineker

Regular Season Quiz 18
1. Ryan Giggs
2. Sylvain Wiltord
3. Mark Viduka
4. Blackburn Rovers
5. Southampton
6. Father
7. Once
8. Gordon Strachan
9. 2002/03
10. False
11. David Unsworth
12. A goal kick
13. Barnsley
14. Marcel Desailly
15. Southampton
16. Hakan Sukur
17. Henning Berg
18. David Seaman
19. Four
20. Five
21. Bradford City
22. Cameroon
23. Wolverhampton Wanderers
24. Gary Kelly

25. Aston Villa
26. Arsenal
27. Coventry City
28. Ipswich Town
29. 2000/01
30. First season
31. Nottingham Forest
32. Senegal
33. Nine
34. Arsenal
35. David Seaman, Alex
    Manninger, Richard Wright
36. Queens Park Rangers
37. Blackburn Rovers
38. Crystal Palace
39. Manchester United
40. Sheffield Wednesday
41. True
42. Wimbledon, Everton
43. 3039
44. Ewood Park (Blackburn Rovers)
45. Manchester United
46. Newcastle United (Elena
    Marcelino)
47. Italy
48. Sunderland
49. Chelsea
50. Manchester City

Regular Season Quiz 19
1. Wimbledon
2. Robbie Fowler
3. Turkey
4. Wallace
5. Leicester City
6. Eric Cantona
7. Nottingham Forest
8. Ipswich Town
9. Newcastle United
10. The Professor

11. Kaspar Schmeichel
12. Goalkeeper
13. Chelsea
14. Everton
15. Wendy Toms
16. Newcastle United
17. Howard Wilkinson
18. La Liga
19. Manchester United
20. Primrose
21. Fulham
22. Francis Benali
23. Wes Brown
24. Andy Cole
25. Gordon Strachan
26. David Seaman
27. Ray Wilkins
28. Whistles
29. Arsenal
30. Portsmouth
31. His shoulder
32. Leeds United
33. West Ham United
34. Robert Pires
35. Bolton Wanderers
36. Blackburn Rovers
37. Liverpool
38. Ruud van Nistelrooy
39. David James
40. Fulham
41. Eric Cantona
42. Leeds United
43. Gianfranco Zola
44. Efan Ekoku
45. Matthew Le Tissier
46. Tottenham Hotspur
47. Chelsea
48. Crystal Palace
49. Laurent Blanc
50. Scott Parker

1. Nine
2. Peter Reid and Mick McCarthy
3. Crystal Palace
4. Wimbledon
5. None
6. Sam Allardyce
7. Wimbledon and Tottenham Hotspur
8. Thirteen
9. Newcastle United
10. Crystal Palace
11. Three
12. Southampton, Coventry City
13. Nottingham Forest
14. Everton
15. Swindon Town
16. Eidur Gudjohnsen
17. Score a penalty against Manchester United
18. Nick Culkin
19. Manchester City and Everton
20. Queens Park Rangers
21. Lucas Radebe
22. Radostin Kishishev
23. Lee Dixon
24. George Burley
25. 2000/01
26. Coventry City, Manchester City, Bradford City

27. Claude Makelele
28. 27
29. Brian Deane
30. Manchester City
31. Coventry City
32. Crystal Palace, Tottenham Hotspur, Aston Villa, Nottingham Forest, Sheffield Wednesday
33. Shaun Bartlett
34. 6%
35. Queens Park Rangers
36. Dave Beasant
37. Slovakian
38. Sir Alex Ferguson
39. Andrei Kanchelskis
40. Franck Quedrue, Wayne Quinn
41. Karel Poborsky
42. Paul Rachubka (sold to Charlton in 2002)
43. Gianluca Vialli
44. John Burridge
45. Ecuador
46. £500,000
47. Sergei Rebrov
48. Queens Park Rangers
49. Paul Merson
50. Peter Crouch